DATE DUE

Look, Listen and Trust

A Framework for Learning through Drama

George Rawlins

Jillian Rich

PLAYERS PRESS, Inc.
P.O. Box 1132
Studio City, CA 91614-0132

3-30-95   17.00 6+T

LOOK, LISTEN and TRUST

ISBN 0-88734-618-9
Library of Congress Catalog Number: 91-51056

PLAYERS PRESS, Inc.
P. O. Box 1132
Studio City, CA 91614-0132

First published 1985, United Kingdom

Printed in the U.S.A.

Library of Congress Cataloging-in-Publication Data

Rawlins, George.
    Look, listen, and trust : a framework for learning through drama /
George Rawlins, Jillian Rich.
        p. cm.
    ISBN 0-88734-618-9 : $16.95
    1. Drama in education.   I. Rich, Jillian.   II. Title.
PN3171.R35   1992
371.3'32--dc20   91-51056
                                                                CIP

Contents

Look

Listen

Trust

Acknowledgement

The authors and publishers are grateful for permission to reproduce an extract from *Under Milk Wood* by Dylan Thomas, published by J. M. Dent & Sons, Ltd.

Introduction

> We cannot use number to solve interesting problems until we have
> to some extent mastered number itself; no more can we use
> drama to understand or experience history or bible stories or
> literature until we have experienced and mastered certain basic
> aspects of drama itself. Ultimately drama is a valuable tool, but
> first must be fashioned.
>
> Brian Way (1967)

This book is for the many teachers of all age groups who wish to use
dramatic method in their teaching, but find it difficult to begin or have
been unsatisfied with the results they have achieved so far. Specialist
teachers, too, may find that the progressively arranged exercises serve to
jog their memories and provide new material for them to try.

No Maths teacher would hand 'A' level problems to a first-year class.
In Drama the learning process is less easily confined, and frequently we
ask for too much, too quickly. Drama lessons fail, time and again,
because pupils have insufficient pre-experience – and thus insufficient
confidence – to deal with the situation in which they are placed by the
teacher. They are, so to speak, required to swim before they've got used to
the water, and the results are unnerving for pupil and teacher alike.

Students need the confidence that comes from having practised basic
skills before they can become involved in more advanced Drama
sessions. And, of course, this applies to pupils of all ages – from First
School to Further Education. The older the student, the more important
the confidence-building becomes.

Over the past fifteen years there has been a rapid increase in Drama as
a timetabled subject in schools. Good teachers have always used drama
but now there is a slot on most timetables where Drama is to be taught.
This has brought obvious advantages – a room for Drama, specialist
teachers, heads of department, and examinations in Drama to secure the
respectable status of Drama/Theatre Arts in schools. All to the good!
Those of us working in education have fought hard for it; but, at the same
time, a certain mystique has grown up around Drama and the Drama
teacher. With Drama as the umbrella-title covering a wide range of
therapeutic, dramatic and sophisticated theatrical activities, it is easy to
forget that, in the first instance, drama is a basic method of learning that
has grown out of *play*.

Play is within everyone's experience – make-believe adventures to test
nerve and muscle power, and release physical and emotional energy;

domestic scenes to come to terms with an adult way of life; rituals exploring sexuality, danger and death; secret gang games where relationships within the group and trust and truthfulness are all important; the excitement of running, swinging, singing, chanting, rhythm and repetition; games to satisfy curiosity, inviting questions, requiring decisions; games to test physical control and coordination; to stretch listening and observation powers; to develop intellectual and creative skills; and manipulative games exacting great concentration and sensitivity.

No educationalist would dispute that children at play are learning about themselves and their environment, practising social behaviour and organising their thoughts into language. This same discovery of life through imaginative play, the testing of new roles and the working out of fantasies in the safe form of the game are at the heart of all educational drama. But the qualities of sincerity and absorption typical of the young child's play must be retained if Drama is to be an effective therapy or teaching tool. Happily, most young children play naturally, although an adult can usefully focus attention on a particular aspect by providing facilities or stimulus. But the older child or adult is likely to be inhibited, to consider himself or herself too *old* to play, and they cannot be expected to put themselves at risk, to lose themselves in a situation which would seem to be far from safe, without help and encouragement.

If we look back to the games of childhood, many of them involve listening or looking carefully. All require total commitment to the game in hand and a self-imposed discipline to play according to the rules. This combination of increased awareness and sensitivity, self discipline and trust and, above all, total absorption, is what we have to recreate if classroom Drama, at any level, is to work.

The exercises and games in this book aim to harness the natural desire to play so that it becomes a driving force for the learning process. We wish to stress that working through exercises is not 'doing drama'. The exercises aim to build the habit of concentration and to create an atmosphere of mutual trust, essential in any learning situation.

Many of the exercises have obvious imaginative developments which lead to Drama. Others may be adapted and used effectively in Science, Humanities, Art or English lessons. Some are helpful control-factors, burning up excess energy or focusing attention for a quiet activity. Many take only five minutes and may be worked in the minimum of space, thus making profitable use of odd moments during the day.

All the activities have been tested in many different teaching situations with a wide range of abilities and age groups. Learning to use the senses and to communicate effectively, know no age barriers, and a little commonsense adaptation will take the same sequence from pre-school playgroup to management training course.

However, just one word of warning: repeated exercises without development, worked in a just-passing-the-time frame of mind, will be counter-productive. The germ of life in each sequence will die in time and the blossoming of experience that might have been will be lost!

The essence of the activities in *Look, Listen and Trust* is active personal discovery and development. All activities are inclusive of all who wish to take part and may be interpreted at many levels. For the student of any age, they build a habit of concentration and sensibility, and extend essential communication skills. For the teacher, they provide a *safe* structure to build upon – a framework in which teacher and class are free to create.

How to use this book

The skills that contribute to readiness for learning are considered under three headings:

observation skills *Look*
listening skills *Listen*
personal awareness and confidence and the ability to work
    with others *Trust*

These areas link and overlap, and experience in one will be evident in the approach to another. Most sequences primarily concerned with one skill draw to a lesser extent on another, and practice in observation or listening is frequently used to develop personal awareness and trust. So, the divisions 'Look', 'Listen', and 'Trust' are somewhat arbitrary, serving mainly to aid identification of the exercises and stress the essential areas of skill, forming the foundation for learning.

'Look', 'Listen', and 'Trust' are divided into closely linked sub-sections. 'Building the Habit' pages contain certain basic activities that should be considered first. Otherwise, sections are of equal importance and may be used in any order. On the right-hand pages you will find 'pre-experience exercises', arranged in order of difficulty. It is *not* intended that the whole section should be worked in one lesson. The activities may be spread over many weeks or, even, years. However, the exercises are arranged progressively, each contributing to the sensitive handling and understanding of the next.

Opposite the exercises, you will find developments and games. The developments use dramatic motivation to explore the skills and concepts previously experienced in the exercise section. They are not progressive and may be tackled in any order, providing that pre-experience has been selected from the facing page. As you work the exercises, many more developments will be evident to you and your class. With so many active minds to draw upon, you will never run out of ideas!

The games rely on adequate pre-experience from the exercise section if they are to be played with depth and conviction. Once learnt, they pass into the repertoire and can be used at any time. Repetition will bring its own refinements and rewards. Played with commitment, they form excellent starters or make good use of moments that might otherwise be wasted at the end of a lesson. The sincerity and absorption typical of the young child's play is recaptured most easily in game form. Children relax as they play. Games generate interest and enthusiasm. They're fun. Many hold the beginnings of role play, others promote a love of sounds and words. Used skilfully, they provide a focus for a particular experience. Remember, though, that relaxed is not 'lethargic'. Fun does not mean 'undemanding'.

The Appendix contains three longer sequences drawing on varied experience gained in *Look, Listen and Trust* and gives an indication of how sequences may be combined and developed.

Style and terminology

On the whole, sequences are presented in a direct command style. A quick read-through should indicate whether instructions are intended for class or teacher!

Pairs (A and B)
It is always helpful to dub pairs 'A' and 'B'. It aids exposition and avoids hesitation at the beginning of a sequence. With young children or an inexperienced class you may need to organise and check the process by asking 'Hands up A's. Hands up B's'. With experience, students will be able to agree who is A or B instantly, even without talking.

Circles
The *size* of the circle should be determined by the teacher. Exposition is simpler and it is sometimes easier to control one large circle, but smaller circles enable exercises to be experienced in greater depth and encourage a degree of involvement that may be difficult to achieve in a large circle.

Circles have an equalising and unifying influence. It's a *safe* grouping. Everyone has a like place and is part of the whole experience. Eye contact is easy and conversation can flow naturally across and around the circle.

Planned improvisation
This suggests discussing and planning an improvisation in groups and sharing it with other people in presentation. Groups may range from pairs to a whole class. This form of Drama is useful for older children and Drama groups. Young children are naturally more spontaneous in their approach. It provides valuable opportunities for quick decision-making and language-flow at the planning stage; practising and observing leadership and cooperation within the group in rehearsal; and artistic endeavour in the presentation when sound and light, levels and costume may be used. Beware of showing-off and stereotype plays that are designed as vehicles for one or two people.

In most cases, the real value of *planned* improvisation is in the planning stage. Many times you may feel that it is unnecessary to 'present' the pieces. The impro has already been acted out in the minds of the participants and an account of what would have happened serves just as well. This decision may be left to the groups. However, if you decide to present the work, make sure that the available time is shared between the class. A promise to find time next lesson for the group caught by the bell isn't acceptable. The 'play' and enthusiasm – and goodwill – of the group will be dead by then!

Older students, in particular, enjoy the challenge of presentation, and should have the opportunity to test their ability to communicate with their audience. When sharing work, require the improvisation to be presented tersely and efficiently ('freeze in opening positions – now begin' is a useful sequence) and insist upon the highest standards of 'audience' behaviour. Sharing is a two-way activity!

As a general rule, avoid using too many props (chairs, tables, cups, etc.). They tend to distract from the essence of the action, and the upheaval and noise of mass furniture removal destroys the atmosphere of the lesson.

As groups grow in confidence and the spirit of 'give and take' in improvisation is accepted, they will become less dependent on lengthy planning sessions and will improvise spontaneously within a loose structure.

Spontaneous improvisation

This implies working an improvisation without previously discussing the plot. Reactions are spontaneous and there is no pre-arranged ending or outcome. This form of improvisation demands a high degree of personal and group awareness, quick imagination, the ability to 'think on your feet', cooperation and a selfless quality that puts the development of the improvisation before personal considerations. Guard against 'sending up' or deliberate 'blocking' of ideas which will quickly undermine the concentration and involvement essential in this style of working.

Spontaneous improvisations can be worked progressively from a circle grouping (one person starts, others join in), or interaction between groups can be arranged with slight contrivance by the teacher. The improvisation may be completely free or suggestions for character or activity may be fed in by the teacher who will sometimes wish to work 'in role'. Frequently spontaneous impro is used after role-play exercises to test and develop characterisation. Spontaneous improvisations are usually followed by discussion and are never repeated.

Teaching styles

There is no 'best way' to teach drama. However, it is well to remember that the greater part of teaching is by example. If the skills of listening, of sensitivity to others, and of awareness of all aspects of communication that we aim to develop in our students are evident in the teacher, the right ambience for learning will exist.

Look

Games using the technique of giving a description

Wanted could obviously be worked as a written exercise. Airport is an expanded version of Wanted, using the whole group and with scope for development in improvisation.

Wanted

(a) Someone describes another member of the class – the 'Wanted' person. Obviously, this must be done without looking at the person and giving the game away. The first to 'put the handcuffs on' the right suspect is the next one to describe a 'Wanted' man or woman.

(b) Instead of describing a member of the class, choose a celebrity as your Wanted person. When someone thinks they know the identity of the celebrity, they say, 'In the name of the law, I arrest ....' If they're wrong, the reply is, 'Release him/her!' If they're right, the response is, 'Lock him/her up!'

Airport   Divide into groups of about six. Take one person out of each group to form a team of airport security officers. The others are all travellers.

Each group of travellers decides on a person (from any group) who must be detained on passing through the departure gate. They agree on the description of this person that is to be given to the security officer.

Meanwhile, the airport officials are setting up two or three departure bays (depending on the size of the group).

A nominee from each group goes to one of the officers and passes on the description of the Wanted person.

Airport officials now gather as a group and compare notes.

Travellers work in character collecting their luggage, discussing journeys, holidays, etc. and, on a signal from the airport staff, begin to queue in the bays arranged by the officers.

Instruct the officers to let people pass through quickly if they don't recognise them as Wanted. When they are satisfied that they have detained the required number of travellers, check with the original 'informers' to see that they have the right people.

On first playing the game, it's likely that the security staff will presume that all of the Wanted people are detained on smuggling charges. Discuss other reasons for detaining or wishing to contact a person and develop in improvisation.

Simple descriptive tasks to reveal how unobservant most of us are, and to encourage alertness and retentive observation.

1 Sames and differences

Find someone who takes the same size shoes as you do. Find someone whose hands are the same size as yours. Find someone the same height, but with different colour hair. Find someone whose favourite colour is the same as yours, etc.

Find someone with any two 'sames' and any two 'differents'. This one creates initial confusion! You can treat it as a simple observation exercise but, if you broaden the scope, children quickly realise that with a little discussion most people can find two 'sames' and two 'differents' in common!

Use as an 'ice-breaker', a fast warm-up exercise, or to create random groups for improvisation.

2 Observation tests

(a) **The room** Working individually, look around the room and try to take in every detail. Close eyes. Teacher is now going to ask the class questions: 'What colour is the door?', 'What colour are my shoes?', 'How many windows are open?' Each person thinks of the answers and then opens eyes to check.

(b) **Partners in the room** Work as for (a) but now partners test each other.

(c) **People in the room** Sit with a partner. A and B. Work as for (b) but concentrate on the people in the room more than on the decor and objects. A's close eyes. A will be expecting his partner to ask him to describe or give the whereabouts of someone in the room. Instead, ask A to describe his partner B. You'll find that the A's will have concentrated on the other people, and having to describe their partners will come as a great shock to them!

(d) **A visitor** Contrive that a child from another class, or a member of staff, calls in on your lesson with a 'message'. When he or she has gone, ask for a detailed description. Recall the visitor to check.

(e) **The school** Ask questions about the school and immediate environs: 'How many light fittings in the main hall?', 'What is the colour of the head-teacher's carpet?', etc.

Have an 'observation drive'. Ask children to look around the school and think of a question to ask the rest of the class next lesson. Have three or four questions at the beginning or end of the lesson.

Observation games

Changing places is also useful as a name-learning game. (For others see Trust – Name games and mixers, pp. 102–7.)

Changing places Divide the class into two. Half stands in a tight group in the centre of the room. The others spread out to form a circle around them. People in the outer circle close eyes. The inner group *silently* chooses one of its number to change places with someone in the outer circle. He or she does so by 'waking' one of the outer circle with a tap on the shoulder and they change places *silently*. The inner group calls, 'Ready!' and starts counting, '1 – 2 – 3...' People in the outer circle open eyes. As soon as someone knows what change has been made, *that person sits down*. The count stops, and he's asked the *names* of the *two* people involved. If he's wrong, the count continues until someone comes up with the right answer. Groups change places and see who can discover the change in the shortest count.

Once the game has been learnt, and the discipline of *sitting down* to answer accepted, play with 2 changes, then 3, 4, 5! The person who sits must give the names of *all* the people involved.

Instruments of the orchestra Sit in a circle. Everyone chooses an instrument to play. One person moves into the centre of the circle with his instrument and the orchestra starts to 'play'. Hum a well-known tune or work to taped music. Suppose the person in the centre is playing the violin. At any time he can change to another instrument that is being played in the circle – say, the piccolo. At this point, the piccolo player must take over playing the violin. If the central player wants to change his piccolo for a drum, the drummer must take over the piccolo, and so on. If a player fails to notice that the central player has 'taken' his instrument, they change places.

(f) **Journeys**   Ask children to make the journey from home to school, or from one point in the school to another, in their minds. Encourage recall of detail. Recall sounds and smells as well as the things you see. Sit with a partner and tell him about your journey. He may question you to extract more details. Change over.

3 Back-to-back descriptions

(a) Work in pairs. A and B. Stand facing your partner and study each other in detail – clothes, colour of eyes, length of fingernails, jewellery, etc. Now turn back-to-back. B asks questions about himself or herself. A responds. Change over.

(b) Work a similar sequence but, this time, A must describe B without the aid of prompting questions.

4 What's the difference?

Stand facing a partner, about 1 metre apart. Look at your partner and remember every detail of his or her clothing. Turn back to back and make a slight alteration to your clothes. On a given signal, face each other and 'detect' what changes have been made.

Progress to several changes. Encourage children to be increasingly subtle, e.g. a ring moved from one finger to another, a shoelace tied differently.

5 What's new?

(a) **Hands**   Sit with a partner. Look carefully at your own hands for blemishes and marks, particularly new ones. Point out these marks to a partner and explain how they were caused.

(b) **The room**   Look for any changes in the room since you were last in it – different placing of furniture, arrangement of wall displays, marks on the floor, on paintwork, on ceiling. Discuss your findings with a partner.

(c) **What's been moved?**   Sit in a space, eyes closed. Touch one person who gets up and walks quietly about the room, moving one object. He or she sits down again. Eyes open. What's been moved?

Developments

What's new?   Set an unexpected or unusually placed object in the room, e.g. an unusual hat on a coat hook, a broomstick in the corner, a 'message' in someone's desk, etc. Wait until someone notices it, then develop a spontaneous improvisation!

Hand maps   Work in pairs. Trace a journey across your palm from the end of your thumb to the 'treasure' at the tip of your little finger. Use your hand as the map and follow the contours and lines. Cross 'rivers', travel along 'roads', climb 'hills', observe other 'landmarks', 'swampy areas', 'barren upland', etc. Change over. Now use your partner's hand as the map. How different is the journey going to be?
Make the journey across the floor of the hall.

Giving a description   Think of situations when an accurate description is required – meeting a stranger off a train, tracing a missing person, identifying a suspect, reporting the sighting of a UFO or the Loch Ness monster.
Work in pairs (interviewer/interviewee) on an imaginary situation and aim to obtain as full a description as possible. The interviewer will need to question his partner carefully so that no points are overlooked. To encourage listening and remembering, and to 'fix' the description, both partners should re-cap from time to time.
Share the description with the rest of the class. Other people may also have seen who or whatever it was, and be able to add their observations. The object here is to work *together* to extend the invented description.

(See also Building descriptions and stories, p. 149.)

(d) **Indian file** A number of 'Indians' 'war-dance' quickly round the room and out of the door. They return in a different order. Who can spot the changes? Start with about six Indians and increase numbers gradually.

(e) **Treasure hunt** Before the lesson, place some objects or 'clues' unobtrusively around the room, e.g. six coins, or milk bottle tops, words that make a sentence, or various objects that must be discovered. Working individually or in pairs, children secretly look for the objects, but may not move them or indicate their position to others. Set a time limit and then discuss the findings. With young children you may provide rhyming clues:

'You're looking for something that rhymes with block
Two hands and a face, it must be a ...'

'You're looking for something that rhymes with bee
If there's a key hole, there should be a ...'

or give anagrams as clues.

Extend this into a treasure hunt around the school or, better still, outside.

Developments in improvisation

Coloured gels in spotlights   Work with three spotlights gelled up in the primary colours – red, green and blue. Create a pool of light in each colour. Use as a stimulus for movement, language, improvisation. Light an area with red and green. Most people are surprised that red and green light make yellow! What happens if you mix the three primaries?

Try some shadow work. Use the three primary colours arranged behind a screen or stretched sheet, with your actors working between the lights and the screen. They will be fascinated by the colours in the penumbra of their shadows, and the magical effects that can quite easily be achieved.

Colour groups   Allow class to group themselves under colours – red, green, blue, yellow, purple. They become 'the Red people', 'the Green people', and so on. In group discussion decide on the important characteristics of that race or section of society, and the image that it wishes to present to the world. Ask each colour group to rehearse a national anthem and a national dance to perform at the Inter-colour festival!

For development see Appendix, p. 180.

1 Touch and return

Sit in a space. Touch something red/green/yellow. Return to personal space and sit down.

Use as a fast warm-up, or as a slower-paced exercise similar to those in Spatial orientation (Individual work), p. 165.

2 Looking for colour

Sit with a partner and work together.

Choose an *unlikely colour* and look for examples of that colour in the room.

Choose a *common colour* and find the most unexpected patch of that colour, or the smallest speck of that colour in the room.

Try to count the number of different shades and tones of any one colour.

Report findings to the rest of the class.

3 Naming colours

(a) Take any reasonably large area of plain colour. Find an original and highly descriptive name for it, e.g. an acid yellow might be called 'crocodile's eye'.

Use trade colour cards for a similar exercise.

(b) Think about the way we frequently describe colour - buttercup yellow, pillar box red, sea green, sky blue, etc. Think of as many of these common descriptions as possible and list them under headings - 'accurate and apt, leaving no doubt about the colour in mind', 'gives a fair idea', 'vague'.

4 Associations

(a) Sit in a circle. Play a word-association game, returning to the key colour after each association, e.g. blue - sky - blue - bell - blue - uniform - blue - jazz - blue - etc.

(b) Consider the images associated with any given colour, e.g. red - danger - passion - flamboyance - importance. What are the roots of these associations?

Colour-coded story Drawing on your experience of colour associations, work out a story that starts Red, becomes Blue, then turns Purple, and finally changes to Black.

Colour-coded personalities Use a colour as a key to each personality in a group improvisation, e.g. a true-blue, a green-horn, a yellow-belly, a red-under-the-bed! Throw in a rainbow personality and the inevitable chameleon.

Set a variety of situations, e.g.

a family deciding how to spend a windfall;
the PTA committee organising an end-of-term outing;
an inquiry on a proposed motorway scheme or local pollution problem
the survivors of an air crash coping on a desert island.

For more ideas, see Character briefs, p. 12.

Or devise a street in which the Browns, the Greens, the Whites, the de Silvers, the Greys – all with distinct family personalities – live next door to each other.

(c) Think of expressions that include colour: in the pink, in the red, feeling blue, green-fingered, silver-tongued, etc. What do they mean? Are they apt? If you like, play this as a charades game – one group choosing an expression to act out, the others guessing it.

Think of an original expression using a colour, and act that out, e.g. What do you suppose 'purple-shouldered' means? Or 'khaki-brained'? Or 'to be out in the beige'?

(d) Choose a colour. Sit with a partner. A and B. A has one minute to persuade B that his colour is best! Change over. If both partners happen to choose the same colour, try to outdo each other extolling the virtues of the chosen colour!

(e) **Colour and texture**   Consider how we associate texture with colour, e.g. The plush of velvet has a rich, red feel, the coarseness of hessian is drab brown, etc. (See Exploring textures – Group work (b) p. 117.)

Developments in improvisation

Shape party   Personify shapes, e.g. How do Rounds move? What sound do Rounds make? What about Diamonds? Or Asterisks?
   When ready, have a Shape party!
   (See Parties, p. 111; Drawing sound, p. 59.)

Shape groups   Set up a sequence similar to the extended exercise on Colour given in the Appendix, using a selection of shapes – the Rounds (earth mothers?), the Squares (predictable conformists?), the Diamonds (sharp and to the point, no doubt!), the Parallelograms (easily swayed?), the Octagons (many-faced!). Ask the class to write the character briefs, and develop in improvisation.

Character briefs   Work in groups of 5: A, B, C, D and E.

   A is crooked
   B is straight
   C is sharp
   D is blunt
   E is rounded

Set a variety of situations, e.g.

   A group of friends planning a party
   People who happen to be in the supermarket
   A team from an advertising agency launching a new product
   A touring theatre company setting up in a new venue
   Colleagues in the motor trade discussing a business venture

Develop in improvisation.

1 Looking for shapes

Sit with a partner and work together. Look around the room for circular or round things (the door knob, the light bulb, the wheel on the piano, a drawing pin head, etc.). Count how many you can see. Report findings to the rest of the class.
Repeat with straight lines, irregular edges, squares, triangles.
Are there any 6-sided or 8-sided shapes in the room?

2 Cut-outs

Prepare a number of different shapes, cut out of card. Lay them on a table or, better still, attach them to a board. Class looks at the shapes. Eyes closed. You remove one of the shapes. Open eyes. Which shape is missing?
Now set the following problems and allow the class to experiment in groups.

(a) Is it more difficult to discover the missing shape if the pattern of the other shapes is changed as well?

(b) What happens if we introduce colour? Suppose each shape is a different colour. Do you first think of the colour that's missing, or the shape? Suppose several shapes in the selection are the same colour. What effect does this have on your memory?

(c) If the shapes differ considerably in size, what do you notice first – the size, or the shape that's missing? Is it easier to remember big shapes or small shapes?

(d) Suppose there are several cut-outs of some of the shapes. Does this make it more difficult to find the missing shape?

(e) What is the maximum number of cut-outs you can display before it becomes impossible to pick out the missing shape?

When experiments are completed, report findings to the rest of the class.

3 Associations

(a) **Character description** Think about the way we use shape in character description. Why do we say 'He's a square'? What do we suggest by a 'rounded personality', 'straight', 'sharp', 'narrow-minded', 'on the level', 'twisted', 'crooked', 'blunt'?

(b) *Emotional response* What is your emotional response to certain shapes? Look at a rectangle. Does it suggest a house, a cage, safety, space? A circle might suggest a flower, an egg, a head, the sun, etc.

Variations on Kim's game

(a) Set up a trayful of different objects or shapes. Class looks at tray for a set time. Eyes closed. Remove one object. Open eyes. What is missing?

(b) Remove 2/3/4/5 objects.

(c) Set up a tray of similar objects, e.g. different coloured pencils and pens, assorted dishes, leaves, a selection of make-up, etc. Which pencil/dish is missing?

(d) *Story trays* Set up a trayful of 5 or 6 interesting, unconnected objects. Allow a short time for class to observe and remember what is on the tray. Divide into groups. Each object must be included in a planned improvisation.

Encourage children to assemble their own trays, with one group preparing a memory task or story tray for another. Small groups will generally achieve far greater involvement and allow more opportunity for talk and individual expression.

4 **Pictures**

Look at a picture. (It's worth making a collection of suitable pictures from magazines, post cards of paintings, etc.)

(a) How many round objects can you find? How many angular shapes?

(b) Look for examples of repeated or contrasting shape.

(c) Do you think the pattern of the shapes is haphazard, or has it been designed?

Discuss in groups and report back to the rest of the class.

(For further ideas on using pictures for observation exercises, see Pictures, p. 36; Comic strip, p. 120; Photographs, p. 126.)

Games practising mirroring and copying skills

Who is changing the movement? Stand in a circle. Send one person outside while you pick a 'leader'. The leader begins a simple repetitive movement. Everyone in the circle copies, but aims not to look directly at the leader. When the leader changes his gesture, everyone should change with him. The 'outsider' is brought in to the centre of the circle and has to discover who is changing the movement.

Who is the boss? The principle of this game is the same as 'Who is changing the movement?', but here there is no circle grouping, and the leader or 'boss' chooses an activity or job – say, delivering milk. Everyone copies him. In his own time, he changes to, say, reading the paper. Everyone copies. The 'outsider' must discover who is the boss.

You can allow a completely different activity at each change, or require that all activities be linked to one job or site (lumberjacks in the forest, on a building site, in a laundry). Encourage pairs to work together – sawing trees, folding sheets, etc.

Bush telegraph team game Play in teams of about six. Members of each team stand behind each other, as far apart as possible, facing one way. Teacher stands at the back of the teams. At the start of the game the *back* person in each team turns to face the teacher who slowly and deliberately mimes a semaphore-type signal to be passed down the team. The back person touches the person in front of him who turns and watches him repeat the signal. And so the signal is passed up the line. No team member may turn until tapped by the person behind him, and all team members sit after passing the signal. The first team to return to the teacher with an *accurate* signal is the winner!

Mirroring exercises which develop concentration and empathy between partners. Continue with basic mirror work until arms begin to move above shoulder level – a sign that partners have confidence in each other and are ready for progression.

NB Mirroring is not a competitive exercise. Don't permit partners to race or try to catch each other out! Encourage smooth, flowing movement, and be ready to work in slow motion as necessary. To slow down young children, suggest that movements are made as if under water.

Stand facing a partner about one metre apart. A and B. Suppose that A is looking into a mirror at B, his exact mirror image.

1 Basic mirror work

(a) A lifts his hands, palms to the 'mirror' and moves his arms slowly and smoothly. As A moves, B 'mirrors' the action. Eye focus should be on foreheads, not on hands. Change over so that B is the leader.

(b) **With feeling** Work as for (a) but specify 'A is feeling strong'. Change over. 'Now B is feeling languid'. Try spiteful, thoughtful, generous, tired, nervous, evil, angelic.

(c) **Learnt sequences**
(i) *Eyes closed* A teaches B a short sequence by repeating the same simple pattern of movement until B is familiar with it, and neither partner is leading nor following. Hands must not touch and there should be no sound. At a signal, both partners close eyes, but continue the movement. After a few seconds, call 'Freeze, and eyes open'. Are the partners still together?

(ii) *Back to back* Work a similar sequence, requiring pairs to turn back to back at the signal. Eyes are kept open. This calls for greater concentration to ignore other movements and distractions in the room. At the signal, turn to face each other. Is the movement still synchronised?

(iii) *Revolving mirrors* This time, both partners begin to revolve slowly, keeping the turn in accord with the tempo of their hand movements. Again, eyes are kept open, developing sympathy between partners as they try to keep aware of each other's movements during the revolve.
   Revolving mirrors also works well with groups of three – '*triple mirrors*'.

(iv) *Changing the leader* Work with a group of four or five. One person faces the others who stand in a line as a set of mirrors, each mirroring the one person facing them all. This person teaches a sequence by repetition. When he is satisfied that the sequence is learnt, he slowly moves to one

Concentration/copying games

Start by playing these games with about ten people per circle and graduate to using the whole class.

Clothes basket   Sit in a circle. First person takes off *in mime* something that he is wearing (clothing, jewellery, false eyelashes). He places the article in a 'basket', which he hands to the next person. This person also takes off something and places it in the basket. And so on, round the circle, until the basket is full. When everyone has placed one article in the basket, continue round the circle, but this time the first person takes something *out* of the basket and puts it *on*. No one may pick out his own possession. The 'recipient' makes eye contact with the 'donor' and puts on the article. Work round the circle until the basket is empty. Commend careful observation and memory for detail in the miming of articles, i.e. *left* hand glove with *two* wrist buttons, rather than 'glove'.

Indian names or How!   Sit in a circle. Each person decides on a Red Indian name for himself or herself plus a gesture to illustrate the name (Running Water, White Owl, Grey Bear, Singing Grass, Shining Star). Work round the circle. Each person says 'Howl' (with appropriate Red Indian gesture) 'Me Running Water!' (or whatever the name is, plus gesture). Everyone responds immediately 'How! Running Water' (with appropriate gestures). When all the Indians have given their names, choose one Indian to start. He or she says 'How!' and calls any Red Indian in the circle but, instead of saying the name, just makes the illustrating gesture. The Red Indian who has been 'called' responds to the caller 'How!' (plus gesture of person who called) and continues 'How!' (gesture of the next Indian he or she wishes to call).

Unrelated actions   Sit in a circle. The first person starts by miming an everyday action, e.g. pulling the tab off a can of fizzy drink. The second person repeats this action and adds an unrelated action of his own, maybe sharpening a pencil. The third person repeats both actions and adds another, and so on. On the second time round, each person must add a sound to illustrate his action. Work quickly and encourage exact copying of gesture and sound.

Use the actions as a starter for a planned impro. Each action must be included in a logical story line. The value here lies in the discussion and invention of a suitable story.

Use one group's sound sequence as a 'sound track' for another group. The second group must explain what it thinks is the story behind the sounds!
(See What is happening, p.46.)

end of the line to become a 'mirror', and the 'mirror' at the opposite end takes his place as leader. During this time, the original learnt sequence is continuing. As soon as the new leader is in position he can begin to change the movement and teach a new sequence. When his sequence is learnt he moves to the end of the line and his place is taken by the next 'mirror'.

Encourage full use of the body in this exercise, bending and stretching, and using facial expression.

(d) **Moving mirrors** Work as for (a) but use the whole body and begin to travel very slowly around the room.

(e) **To music** Work to music, letting the initiative pass between partners with no spoken communication.

With an experienced group this is useful as a limber/concentration exercise before starting the lesson.

(f) **Opposite mirrors** A gradually moves into a shape. As he is moving, B moves in the opposite direction. So if A is stretching into a wide, open position, B will be curling into a tight, closed shape. If A smiles, B grimaces. Let the initiative pass between A and B without spoken communication.

Use this exercise as an energetic warm-up with partners jumping into opposite positions. See Levels exercises in Statues, p. 127.

(g) **Grotesques** This is a similar sequence to 'Opposite mirrors'. Suggest that A is looking at his reflection in a distorting mirror. Change over.

Line up the A's as a 'hall of mirrors'. B's walk through, looking at distorted reflections in each mirror. Change over so that B's form the hall of mirrors.

---

2 Shadowing

Work in pairs. A and B.

(a) **Shadows** B is A's shadow. B lies down, his feet touching A's feet, or sits against the wall, so shadow is half on floor, half on wall. A begins to do physical exercise (knee bends, etc.) or gives a 'talk' illustrated with positive, large gestures. Shadow moves accordingly.

Try with two shadows.

(b) **Tracking** B is going to track A, following exactly in his or her footsteps, two or three metres behind and doing exactly what he or she does. If A hears B, A turns round suddenly and B aims to freeze before A can catch him moving. When A has caught B moving three times, they change over.

Development in improvisation

It's useful to have played 'How!' before attempting this more complicated sequence. Both are based on linking gesture to a word and learning by copying.

Survival vocabulary Ask each member of the class to choose just *two* words which will become his 'survival vocabulary'. He will have no other vocabulary apart from these two words! When the words have been chosen, each person adds a gesture to suit each of his words.

Now find a partner and teach your partner your words, so you'll have four words with gestures between you. No general conversation may be used in the teaching process, just repetition of the chosen words.

Proceed with your partner to teach your words and gestures to another pair. Now you'll have the use of eight words.

Finally, move as a foursome to teach your words to another four. Each group should end up with sixteen words and gestures.

These must now be used to form a story or statement. Each word and gesture may be used as many times as proves necessary. Permit normal conversation during the planning stage.

Present the survival scenes.

(c) **Indian hunting party**   Work in teams of five or six as a silent Indian hunting party. Plan the journey first and then set off in Indian file.

(d) **Stepping patterns**   Work in groups of three, A, B and C. Stand side by side. A moves forward three steps in a distinctive way (e.g. hopping, or walking on heels, or dragging feet). B follows, copying exactly, and adds three more steps of his or her own. C follows, copying A's movement, then B's, and then adding three more distinctive steps. A is now six steps behind, so he copies B's pattern, then C's pattern, to catch up, before adding a further pattern. And so on.

Aim for maximum contrast in pace, levels and floor contact in each stepping pattern, and quick and smooth follow-on of repeated movements. This gives a 'wave' effect.

(See Listen – Footsteps, pp. 48–53.)

3   Delayed mirrors

(a) **Facial expression**   Work in pairs. A and B. A begins a sequence of actions (eating a meal, putting on make-up). After each action, B mirrors the movement. The delayed action enables him to observe facial expression and the smallest details of movement.

Try eating a lemon, chewing gum, eating a delicious pudding, smelling burning.

Use slow motion and 'Double it!' (p. 149) to develop detail and concentration.

(b) **Copy the expert**   Sit round in a semi-circle with one 'expert' out in front. The expert begins to demonstrate something he can do confidently (wiring a plug, making pastry, changing a baby's napkin), stopping after each action to allow the others to copy. After the task has been learnt, stage by stage, run a continuous mass mirror sequence, each person being aware of the actions of the others and aiming to keep all movements in unison.

4   Faces

(a) Work in pairs. A and B. A is to mirror B. B slowly 'pulls' a 'mask' over his face. A mirrors the mask. When B is satisfied with his reflection, he relaxes, and then takes the mask off A. Change over.

(b) Work as for (a), but ask A to speak 'in character' before B frees him of the mask.

More advanced improvisation sequences with scope for imaginative character work.

Catch and cure Work in pairs. A and B. Each partner decides secretly to adopt some ailment or affliction, e.g. A might decide that he has an itchy nose, while B might have a stiff knee. They sit together in character and talk about anything except their ailments! As soon as either partner is aware of the other's ailment he can begin to 'catch' it. This 'cures' the original sufferer. So partners end up with each other's problems!

Play a progressive Catch and cure sequence on a circle of 'park benches', with A's moving on after each exchange of ailments.

Discuss how the Catch and cure principle operates on a broader scale (sharing a problem, fast-changing fashions and crazes, exchange of roles). Develop in improvisation.

Mirror, mirror, see my soul! Work in groups of four (two pairs). First pair begins an improvisation – say, 'At the hairdresser's'. It's probably easier to start without speech. After a few seconds, they stop, and the second pair 'mirrors' their actions. First pair repeats the sequence adding speech. Second pair copies action and speech. And so on through a fairly short sequence. Now each pair will have learnt the sequence and, by watching and listening closely, will probably have formed some opinions about the true character and sincerity of its counterpart. Play the sequence again, but this time the mirror image should try to reflect what it thinks would be the *true* thoughts and character of the other pair, rather than copying speech and facial expression exactly. For instance, if the hairdresser says, 'How lucky we had a cancellation and could fit you in!', he might well be thinking, 'So much for my getting home early!' When the customer leaves, she probably says, 'Thank you, that's lovely!' – but does she really mean it?

The hairdresser and client in front of a real mirror works well as a starter for this impro, providing obvious motivation for the 'mirroring' but, of course the 'mirror' is essentially abstract.

5 Throwing faces

Stand in a circle. One person 'puts on' a face. He makes eye contact with someone else in the circle, 'takes off' his face and 'throws it' to his 'contact'. Contact puts on the face, makes eye contact with someone else, and then throws him the face.
(See Eye contact circle, p. 27).

6 Reverse re-play

Work with a partner. A and B. A assumes a broad character and advances towards B (burglar creeping towards safe, footballer taking penalty kick, model on cat-walk, drunk lunging towards bar, etc.). B assumes A's final position and moves back 'reversing' A's movements. Change over.

7 In front of the mirror

(a) Stand in a circle. One person assumes a stance and facial expression. In 'character' he moves and stands in front of a 'mirror' (someone else in the circle). The 'mirror' takes up his pose. When the first person is happy that his mirror image is 'sharp', he relaxes and returns to his place. The mirror image now 'becomes alive' and moves to stand in front of another mirror.

(b) Work as for (a) but require each 'image' to *amend* physique or characterisation en route to the next mirror. Changes may be very subtle, or more obvious additions to develop a character.

8 Mirror speech

Sit facing a partner. A and B. A starts to speak *very slowly*, mouthing words carefully. B concentrates on A's mouth and 'mirrors' the speech so they are both saying the same thing at the same time. Change over so that B is leading. After the first few moments of this exercise you should not be able to tell who is leading, who is following!

Games

Wink murder is a well-known ice-breaker. All people in the circle make quick and humorously-motivated eye contact with each other.
Stand in a circle. Eyes closed. Touch one person who is to be the 'murderer'. Now everyone opens eyes. Choose a 'detective' to stand in the centre of the circle. The murderer kills by winking at his victim who may die a horrible death! How quickly can the detective discover the murderer?

Develop the game by selecting another detective from those still living at the end, and asking him to remember and report how his friends died, i.e. poisoned, stabbed in the back, strangled, etc.
(See Instant reactions, p. 65.)

The haunted house An atmospheric game in which eye contact can have a chilling effect!

Think of some of the things you might find in a haunted house – floor boards that creak, pictures that laugh or follow you with their eyes, suits of armour that move, shutters that fly open, grandfather clocks that strike suddenly.

Practise making ghostly noises and think about some spooky actions to go with the sounds.

Now, choose a 'victim' and send him out of the room. Very quickly the class forms objects *round the walls* of a haunted room. Try to have two children as a squeaky door. Ask each 'object' to decide on a point on the floor which activates its ghostly action and sound. Then, silence and stillness. Dim the lights, and invite the victim in. He comes through the door and, as he walks around the room, different objects come to life momentarily as he steps on their 'activating point'.

Vary the sequence by adding group activities, e.g. when the victim is in one half of the room everyone makes wind noises, or everyone follows him with their eyes, in total silence, for the silent count of twenty when he first comes in, then the noises begin!

Exercises and games which overcome initial reticence about making and holding eye contact, and establish the value of eye contact in communication.

1   What colour?

(a) Sit with a partner. What colour are your eyes? Describe the colour of your *own* eyes to your partner, and then listen as your partner describes your eyes as he or she looks at them. Change over.

(b) Sit in threes. A, B and C. All the Cs are eye-colour scouts! Their job is to organise the rest of the class into eye-colour groups. When they have sorted out all the As and Bs they can work amongst themselves to find which group they belong to. The class will quickly discover that there's more to eye colour than 'blue' or 'brown'!

2   See yourself

Find a partner. Can you see yourself mirrored in the pupils of your partner's eyes? You may need to adjust head angle to catch the clearest image. Can you both see each other?

Now separate and mix, meeting other people. Try not to leave a person until you have achieved an 'eye mirror' with them.

Does the colour of a person's eyes have any bearing on their reflective quality?

3   Holding contact

Sit facing a partner, about one metre apart. Look down at the floor. On a signal, both partners look up and make eye contact. Hold for the count of three. Don't try to stare each other out. Use a 'soft focus' and look into your partner's eyes without emotion or communication.

As group gains experience, extend contact time up to count of twenty.

4   Holding contact and moving

Hold 'soft' eye contact with a partner, and move together *very* slowly around the room. Try to keep the same distance apart and develop an empathy so that neither of you is consciously leading or following.

At first, don't have too many pairs moving at once, otherwise eye contact will inevitably be broken to avoid collisions.

Communication games

Lively eye contact and facial expression are called for in these games. They are also excellent mouth and projection exercises, developing the strength and flexibility essential in good, clear speech.

Shopping lists   Work with a partner. A and B. Stand at opposite sides of the room facing each other. Imagine that A is inside the supermarket while B is on the pavement outside. A cannot hear B, so B must 'mouth' and 'mime' the items he wants bought in the supermarket – eggs, milk, sweets, baked beans, etc. As soon as A gets the message, he gives the 'thumbs up' and the shopping list continues. Chat to see if the messages were correctly received. Change over. Have a competition to see which pair can pass and remember most messages!

Develop by requiring more detail in the lists. 'Eggs' or 'sweets' is no longer good enough. The shopper needs to know quantity, quality, colour, brand, etc., i.e. 'half a dozen, size 3, brown eggs'.

Try a fantastic hypermarket where anything can be bought – anything from a Rolls Royce to roller skates for a circus elephant!

TV with no sound   Work in groups and, using strongly mouthed words and positive gesture, present a television programme with no sound.

You could precede the programme with an announcement apologising for nationwide loss of sound and assuring the audience that the actors will ensure that this minor technical fault does not detract from their enjoyment of the programme.

Maybe, prepare a captions board stating the problem!

5 Eye contact circle

Stand in a circle. One person starts. He makes eye contact with someone else in the circle and throws him an imaginary ball, 'Catch'. That person makes eye contact with another, and then throws the ball, 'Catch'.
Establish that eye contact must be made before the ball is thrown. Start slowly, and then work up speed to demand more urgent, intense eye contact.
This eye-contact technique serves to increase involvement and concentration and can be usefully employed in many circle games and exercises.

6 Eye communication

(a) **Flashing messages**   Sit facing a partner, as in Holding contact. Look down at the floor. This time, on the signal, one of you is going to communicate with the other – to flash one word with your eyes. Give a choice of Love, Hate, or Fear.
Allow the eye contact to be held for about five seconds before partners look at the floor again. Then discuss which message was passed.
Change over. Try Pain, Admiration, or Mistrust.

(b) **Masked**   Cover the face with a simple mask in which small eye holes have been cut. Repeat exercise (a). Is it possible to receive the message from the eyes alone?
Enlarge the eye holes slightly and try again. Consider how important the muscles round our eyes are in communication.
Cut the mask to reveal the mouth. Can 'mouth messages' (smiles, sneers, etc.) be misunderstood if you can't see the eyes? Experiment with simple paper masks.

7 What am I looking at?

(a) **In the room**   Work in pairs. A and B. A looks intently at a chosen spot (part of the pattern on the curtains, a small object in the room, a spot on the floor). B moves and aims to touch the spot or object that A is looking at. Change over.

(b) **Imaginary**   A looks at something (a high wire artiste, a bee, a boring book, a difficult puzzle, the culture of a sinister biological weapon, etc.). B aims to tell him what he is looking at. Change over.
Run a group sequence. Sit in circles in small groups of about six or eight. In turn, pick up a 'letter' – the morning post. This can contain good news, infuriating news, sad news. It might be a dreaded summons or a

Prisoners' exercise yard   Find a partner. A and B. A's make an inner circle, B's make an outer circle. A's start walking to the right. B's start walking to the left. So circles are moving in opposite directions.

Each prisoner A needs to pass a *silent* message to his partner. Suggest 'Time of escape', 'Rendezvous point', 'Get-away vehicle'. Set a time limit. Don't allow dawdling or any obvious gesture!

Stop and chat. Change over.

The escape   Set up a POW camp situation. Women are in A Block, one side of the room. Men are in B Block, on the opposite side. Extract one 'guard' to watch over them!

The girls have discovered the best day, time and rendezvous point for the planned break-out. The boys must decide on the equipment and provisions that will be needed to make the escape. These points are agreed on, in their separate cell blocks, at the beginning of the exercise.

This information must be shared during the brief exercise period in the centre of the room. The guards can send anyone seen acting suspiciously back to the cell!

Call 'End of exercise period. Back to quarters.' Both groups, still under occasional supervision from the guards, recap on the plan of escape.

You may need a second exercise period in which groups can pass any messages necessary for the completion of the plan – equipment collected, times confirmed, etc.

Run the exercise to its logical conclusion by attempting to make the breakout.

Discuss the effectiveness of the communication between and within groups, and consider how the messages might have been delivered more efficiently.

win on the pools, a love letter, an illegible letter, an invitation, a poison-pen note, an amusing, chatty letter with cuttings and snap shots. The rest of the group watch the initial reaction to the letter and then develop the scene in spontaneous improvisation.

A reading of W. H. Auden's 'Night Mail' could aptly follow this sequence.

(c) **Looking with different eyes**   This time the imaginary sights are looked at from different points of view, e.g. an ink stain on the carpet might be looked at by the child who has spilt the ink, the mother/headteacher who has just bought the carpet, the professional cleaner checking the suitability of a solvent.

8 Eye control

Work in pairs. A and B. A is master, B is servant. Master fixes 'hard' eye contact on servant, and commands him, using eye control only, to move in a certain direction, to fetch a chair, to pick something up off the floor, etc.

Change over.

Note that eye control is the only means of communication open to some people. How would you feel in this situation?

Related games that may run on into spontaneous improvisation

Joining-in game Sit in a circle. Prepare a number of cards: 'You are in the library', 'down a coalmine', 'in the supermarket', 'at the races', 'in church', 'at the fairground', 'swimming the channel', etc. Show one to the first person, who moves into the centre of the circle and reacts in mime according to the instruction on the card. As soon as the others guess where he or she is, they can join in. When the whole class is working, stop, and ask a few people where they thought they were!

Who and where game Send one person out of the room. Quickly tell the others who they are, where they are and who they are waiting for, e.g. the staff in an operating theatre waiting for the surgeon. They start to work according to their instruction and react as the one waiting outside is brought into their scene. How quickly can this person perceive and take over the role that has been allotted to him? There is no need to limit the scene to mime, and verbal clues can become more obvious if the outsider really cannot make out who and where he is.

Try restaurant staff waiting for the health inspector; workers in a factory threatened with closure, hoping to impress the richest man in the world; a wedding party waiting for the best man; gangsters waiting for instructions from their boss.

What's the time? Sit in a circle. One person starts and mimes an action associated with a certain time of day – filing into assembly, cleaning teeth (is it morning or evening?), getting up in the middle of the night on hearing a noise, etc. Does everyone know what the time is?

Try similar sequences:
What am I waiting for?
What are we eating?
What are we watching?
What are we listening to?
What can we smell?
What are we frightened of?
What have I found?

Don't feel that the action must be limited to mime. Develop in progressive improvisation with people from the circle joining in.

Exercises developing close observation and a receptive approach between partners.

1 Advancing

(a) **Basic advancing** Work in pairs. A and B. A starts to mime an everyday action, e.g. washing in the morning. At every progression point in his mime he waits for B to express understanding. If B understands what A is doing, he says 'Advance' and A continues the mime. If B remains silent, A must try to make the action clearer before 'advancing'. Change over.

(b) **Reality into fantasy** Start as for (a), but now A is not tied to the mundane. He may start by filling the wash basin, but then decide to shrink, dive in and take a swim before scrambling up the side to make a meal out of the soap! B watches carefully, telling A to 'advance' as soon as he thinks he understands the action. At the end of each sequence, check to see if B's interpretation was accurate. Maybe it was even more fantastic than A intended.

(c) **Change-over advancing** A starts, but, when he reaches a progression point in his mime, he stops and asks B to 'Advance' for him. B continues and develops the sequence, before handing back to A to 'Advance' again.

(d) **Chain** Sit in a circle. One person starts by miming an action, say, cutting a slice of bread. Next person continues with a logical development - buttering the bread. And so on round the circle.

Encourage imaginative reaction and easy transition from reality to fantasy.

2 Join in and take over

Work in pairs. A and B. A starts to mime doing a job - digging a hole in the road, delivering the milk, frying an egg. As soon as B thinks he knows what A is doing he joins in. When A is satisfied that B is doing the right thing he leaves him working. B quickly finishes that job and starts another one. A joins him. And so on.

Two observation/copying/remembering games

What didn't I do? Work in pairs. A and B. A starts to mime an everyday activity. B watches. A will deliberately 'forget' to do something, i.e. he'll fail to turn the tap off, won't put the lid on the kettle, etc. B must say what he didn't do and then repeat the mime adding the missing action.

Music school Invent a new instrument. Play it in mime. Add the sound it makes. Meet a partner. Teach him how to play your instrument. Exchange instruments and continue.

After instruments have been exchanged several times, stop, and ask one player to give a short recital. Does the inventor recognise his instrument?

Ask for suitable names for the favourite inventions!

3 | Cameraman

Use your hands as a viewfinder on a camera to frame the picture you want in shot. By moving hands away from your face you take a 'close-up'. The nearer you hands are to your eyes, the 'wider' the angle of your shot.

(a) **To music** Work with a partner. A is cameraman. B is model/actor/dancer. Use music. B moves freely. A follows with camera, moving in for close-ups, away for long shots, and experimenting with different camera angles. Change over.

(b) **With a director** Work in threes on a similar sequence. This time you add a director (C). He gives instructions to his cameraman – low/medium/high shot, wide angle, close up on hands, etc. Change over.

(c) **Interpretation** Work with a partner. A and B. A is going to convey an emotion or state of mind with his whole body – grief, impatience, joy, embarrassment. B must use his 'camera' close-up to focus on hands only. Do they tell him what A is feeling? Change over.

Try focusing on feet and, finally, on your partner's back.

(d) **Bird's-eye view** Think of the angles you would use if you wanted to suggest that the scene was being viewed by a cat, a fly on the wall, a worm, a giraffe.

This 'camera' technique can be used in many observation exercises. It requires active participation of the observer and is a useful concentration booster.

Developments in improvisation

Bus queue Form a bus queue. Communicate by stance and expression who you are and what you are feeling. What happens when the bus draws up and the conductor says, 'Only room for *two*, on top!'?

Seven Ages of Man (*As You Like It* Act II, scene 7) Try a 'Seven Ages of Man' bus queue, or waiting room.

The Seven Dwarfs Work in groups of seven. Start by remembering the names and characteristics of the seven dwarfs! Each person in the group should now decide on a name/characteristic for himself. It can be one used in the Snow White story or one he has made up. Choose a task – mundane or extraordinary, i.e. washing the car or, maybe, washing an elephant, which the group must tackle together. The others watch and, at the end of the sequence, name the characters in each group.

Animals Work a similar sequence in which each person takes on the characteristics of an animal.

An introduction to the vocabulary of non-verbal communication. The value of these exercises is in the discussion and exchange of personal experience that must follow them.

1 Moods

Take a simple task and do it in different moods – happy, sad, angry, impatient, bored, etc.

(a) Work in pairs. Can your partner observe what mood you are in?

(b) Work in pairs or small groups, all doing the same job. Each one of you decides on the mood you are in. What effect do the moods have on the group's activity? How does another person's mood influence the way you feel?

2 Images

Working individually, in mime, dress in the morning and walk to work projecting the personal image 'I'm successful', 'misunderstood', 'non-conformist', 'artistic', 'academic', 'down-to-earth', etc.

3 What's in a smile?

Work in pairs to communicate a range of meanings.

(a) **What's in a smile?** Make it cool, warm, artificial, genuine, surprised, alluring, cynical, sneering, etc.

(b) **A nod** Experiment with head inclinations to say 'Go on, I'm listening', 'Yes!', 'I don't believe you', 'I'm thinking about it', 'I'm bored', 'Maybe', 'No!', etc.

(c) **A handshake** Work in pairs and discover if the handshake is a non-communicative formality, or does it say 'I would like to know you better', 'I don't trust you', 'Marvellous to see you again', 'I hope we're going to get on', 'I want to impress you', etc.

(d) **A tap on the door** Listen to people tapping on the door. Do they sound timid, polite, thoughtless, determined, threatening?

(e) **A hand clap** Work as a group and communicate your feelings by clapping – polite acceptance, enthusiasm, cynicism, anger, delirium, boredom.

Games

Pictures   Collect photographs of people. Avoid posed portraits and set-up shots. Go for pictures that have caught the subject unaware of the camera. Look at facial expression, hands, gesture, stance, the position of one person in relation to another, clothes.
Use as starters for discussion or improvisation.

Sitting together   Sit facing a partner. Allow yourselves to relax into similar sitting positions and unobtrusively 'mirror' changes of movement. What effect does this have on the tone of your conversation? You'll probably find it very difficult to argue and keep similar positions.

Work out an improvisation using the technique of 'mirroring' positions as a conscious attempt to create and maintain harmony, e.g. leaning on a bar, a doctor putting a patient at ease, two people in a tea shop.

Confusions   Presume that an alien or group of aliens has joined your community. They are unfamiliar with conventional non-verbal signals, or maybe our signals hold different meanings for them. Consider the comic misunderstandings that might arise. Act out the situation.

(f) **Sitting position** Sit on your own as if nervous, anxious about someone else, uncomfortable but not wishing to show it, comfortable, relaxed, exhausted.

Sit with a partner and discover a range of subtle changes in relationship by varying your sitting positions.

(g) **A touch** Work with a partner. Take his arm and walk with him as if he is older than you, younger than you, as if you need his help, in affection, in respect, in anger, with misgivings, etc. Can you partner feel the difference in touch?

4 Communicating with accepted signals

In groups, confer to build a 'vocabulary' of accepted non-verbal signals.
Can you signal the following?
What about a drink?
Do you smoke?
I'm hungry.
He's crazy!
Keep quiet!
Get lost!
He goes on and on...
Help me!
It's nothing to do with me.
Honestly, it's the truth.
I don't know.
OK.
No luck!

Link the gestures to make a logical sequence. Add a few 'signals' of your own that you think might catch on and pass into our non-verbal vocabulary!

5 Characteristic communication styles

Consider the following communication styles:
standing well apart from each other and shouting
standing close together and talking quietly
using touch and gesture flamboyantly
avoiding all physical and eye contact
hiding emotion behind a fixed smile

Is it possible to indicate a certain personality type by adopting non-verbal behaviour like this? From your own observations, can you add to the list?

What happens when people with conflicting communication styles meet? Experiment, and discuss the misunderstandings that may arise. Contrive and develop a humorous scene based on your observations.

Games

And how is Ethel/Ernest today? Sit in a circle. Ask the first person, 'And how is Ethel today?' 'Ethel' might decide she has a headache and makes the appropriate gesture. Everyone deduces, 'Ethel has a headache!' Continue round the circle, 'And how is Ernest today?' 'Ernest' might fill his lungs with air and flex his muscles! 'Ernest is feeling fit!' etc.

'I have lost my phrase book.' You are a traveller in a foreign country, with no knowledge of the language. You need to communicate the following (for example):

I have lost my phrase book!
I have left my umbrella on the train.
I come out in spots if I eat crab.
I think I have food poisoning.
Where can I buy a cup of tea?

Any phrase book will supply you with more hilarious examples!

Have one person communicating to the rest of the class. Or, for deeper involvement, work in pairs or small groups. One person in each group should be taken aside and told the line he must communicate.

6 Animal behaviour

(a) Think about animal displays – courtship, territorial, maternal. How similar are the human animal's antics?

Start a scene as animals and slowly change into people. Try:

peacocks who evolve into young people wearing fashionable clothes,

apes grooming each other who become mother and child or hairdresser and client,

monkeys swinging through the jungle who change into strap-hanging commuters!

Or work the other way round – from people into animals – for a more biting comment!

(b) Collect a list of words and expressions generally applied to people but derived from the habits of creatures.

What about to be catty, to beaver away, to ape, to fox, to badger, to dog someone's footsteps, to wolf, to hound, to ferret, to be an ass, to crow, to be broody, snake in the grass, birds in their nest.

Listen

Well-known listening games used to develop the habit of careful, sensitive movement

In many cases, given an imaginative setting, they make good starters for improvisation.

Raising ghosts! Everyone lies down on the floor, eyes closed, as 'sleeping ghosts'. Walk quietly and 'raise' one of the ghosts by touching him on his forehead. He opens his eyes, gets up and very quietly raises another ghost by touching him on the forehead. And so on, until, by mutual agreement, there is just one ghost left lying on the floor. The other ghosts form a circle around him and suddenly, altogether, *shout* his name!

Develop as a 'Waking graveyard' story or movement sequence with suitable sound effects!

Or change the 'ghosts' into sleeping outlaws in the forest (Robin Hood's men?) who wake each other silently and group to fire their arrows at the source of danger. Group in a line. Count quietly: one – two – three – four – five – as the bows are prepared, and let the arrows fly on a long onomatopoeic six . . . .

Keys Sit in a *large* circle, facing outwards. Eyes closed. Place a bunch of keys in the centre. Touch one person who opens eyes and tries to pick up the keys and return to his place without being heard.

Pirate's treasure The Pirate King sits on chair in centre of circle with various 'treasures' around him. he 'goes to sleep' – eyes closed! The rest of the class cooperate to see if they can remove treasures without waking the King. If anyone succeeds in getting a treasure, the King must make accusations until he finds the culprit. The most successful 'crew' are the ones who steal most and conceal the theft longest!

Introductory exercises to develop personal calm and stillness and establish the habit of listening.

1 Outside - inside

Sit in a space by yourself. Eyes closed.

(a) Listen to the sounds you can hear coming from *outside* the building. Suppose you didn't know where you were, what could you deduce from listening to the sounds? - nearness of road or railway line, footsteps (adult or children?), animals, etc.

(b) Concentrate on sounds *inside* the building. Listen hard and you may be surprised what you can hear!

(c) Listen to sounds *in the room*. Use Listening to footsteps on p. 49, following exercises in this section to focus attention.

(d) Listen to the sound of *yourself* - your breathing, your slightest movement, even your heartbeat.
Encourage children to practise these listening exercises at home, in town, on the beach, at different times of day, and to share their experience back in class.

2 Pinpointing sound

Sit in a space. Eyes closed.
Walk around the room so that the class gets used to the sound of your footsteps. Then stop. Using the tip of a pencil or your finger nail, gently tap on one spot on any surface in the room. Children point to the spot you are tapping. Encourage them to focus all their attention on the centre of that spot.
Open eyes to check, if you wish.

3 Length of sound

Sit in a space. Eyes closed. Raise right arm.
Listen to one note played on piano, cymbal, chime bar, triangle, Indian bells, etc. Lower hands silently as all reverberations of the sound die away. Listen for the last moment of the sound.

Guards at the gate Five children stand side-by-side in a line so that fingertips just touch. Their arms form the multiple gate. Drop arms and close eyes. Four children start at the other end of the room and must pass through the 'gateways' without being heard. If they hear any sound, 'guards' raise arms to 'close' whichever gate is threatened. Once a gate is shut, the would-be intruder must freeze. The game ends when someone gets through the gate, or all the gates are closed.

Also play this in circle form, with guards forming a circular enclosure around captives.

In groups, prepare a planned improvisation on the theme, 'The guarded gate'. What about three-headed Cerberus guarding the entrance to Hades, or the dragon guarding the golden fleece, or the entry of the Wooden Horse into Troy?

Moving to music games

(a) Move *in time* to the music or beat. When the music stops, freeze.

(b) Listen to the sound (music/percussion/vocal sound/words/etc.) and move *as the sound suggests* (giants/mice/ghosts/or more adult, abstract interpretations). When sound stops, freeze.

(c) Lay hoops, mats, pieces of paper, etc. on the floor. Move 'in character' to sound, as for (b), avoiding obstacles. When sound stops, get inside or on to one of the *'magic areas'*. Listen to the next sound, and change into something else.

(d) Use the 'animals' or 'characters' experienced in (b) and (c) together with their 'sounds' *in a story*. One group can make sounds for another group.

Roundabout Use fairground music. Children move round in a circle, bobbing up and down like horses on a roundabout. When the music stops, they freeze.

With older children specify that horses must be alternately high/low. This imposes an extra discipline and increases demands on children's concentration.

(For more *when the music stops* games, see Pair statues, p. 124; Freeze, p. 125.)

4 High/low notes

Play a number of notes or make sounds. Which was the highest note? Which the lowest? Start with two sounds. Progress to three, four, five. Practise this exercise working in pairs or small groups.

5 Nearest/furthest sounds

(a) Sit in a space. Eyes closed. Use a percussion instrument or clap hands gently as you walk amongst children. Children raise arms if the sound is close to them, lower arms as the sound moves further away.

(b) Working in small groups, sit together, eyes closed. One person gets up and walks around the groups making sounds (percussion, claps, sung notes, speech) at different points in the room. Eyes open. Each group confers and decides which sound was made nearest and which furthest away from it.

6 Soft sounds

(a) Encourage listening to soft sounds – the clock ticking, paper rustling, hands rubbing together, even the proverbial pin dropping!
To break the habit of unnecessarily noisy communication, whisper your own instructions whenever apt.

(b) In pairs, sitting about a metre apart, whisper an instruction/ address/nursery rhyme to your partner. The whisper should be clear and as quiet as possible. The message may not be repeated.
Note, this isn't a Chinese whispers game in which the message may be obscured deliberately, but an exercise to promote clarity of speech as well as sensitive listening.

7 Tone, colour and shape

(a) Use recorded music or create your own. Ask – is it a sad sound? cheeky? awkward? prim? joyful? aggressive? What does the music make you think of – a mood, a picture, a story?
Discuss and develop in groups. See Sound and movement sequences, p. 62.

Imaginative development

What is happening? Prepare a tape of five or six sound effects in story sequence, e.g. car journey/bird song and country atmosphere/a stream/a scream. Play the tape until the class is familiar with it. Divide into groups and make up a sequence to fit the tape. Many stories will fit the same sound sequence. Discuss the variations.

Now, in groups, make up your own short sound sequence, using percussion, objects in the room, voices. Listen to each of the sequences in turn, and ask another group to respond immediately with action to suit the sound. How does their story line compare with the group's original idea?

Encourage groups to be imaginative and inventive in their interpretation of the sounds. They probably know exactly *how* the sound was made, but can they think what it sounds *like* – what it *might* be?

(b) Make different sounds. Use instruments, your own 'sound makers' or recordings. What colour are the sounds? The highest notes on the piano might be silver, the factory siren could be orange, an echoing door slam – navy blue?
Discuss in groups. See Drawing sound, p. 59.

(c) What shapes are different sounds – round, pointed, long and thin, flabby, puffy, bumpy?
Discuss in groups. In groups, make or choose a sound and ask the others to decide on its colour and shape.

8 | How many sounds

(a) **Paper** Sit in pairs. Give each pair a sheet of newspaper.
How many sounds can you make with it, i.e. How many different *methods* of making sounds can you find? (The paper can be crumpled, snapped, scratched, rubbed, stroked, hit, blown across, rolled to form a tube, and torn.)
Listen to the change in pitch as you tear paper at different speeds. Have a slow-tearing race, and a fast-rip race with your partner.
Experiment with different thicknesses of paper and cardboard.

(b) **Sound-makers** Sit in small groups. Give each group a 'sound-maker' – broken percussion, tins, tubes, boxes, almost anything you have to hand. How many different sounds can you make with it?
Start collecting, grouping and modifying sound-makers to form 'rubbish bands'. Use to accompany a song, or make your own music. Choose names for the new instruments.

Listening for footsteps games

How did he do it? Specify a certain number of paces and hops that may be used to get from one set point to another, say, 3 paces and 2 bunny hops. Choose one child to start. He can use the hops and paces in any order he chooses, but must use the number stated. Say, 'Eyes closed!' for the rest of the class and, 'Start!' When he has finished, 'Eyes open!' for the class and, 'How did he do it?' Class responds, 'One hop, three paces, then another hop,' or whatever.

When the children know the game, make it a little more difficult by having *eyes closed* before you pick the child who is to move. So you ask, '*Who* was it?' as well as, 'How did he do it?'

Still pond You need a 'catcher' who works 'blind', and as many 'frogs' in the pond as space will allow. The catcher specifies the maximum number of hops each frog is allowed in order to get out of danger. He stands in the centre, eyes closed, and the frogs move freely till he calls, 'Still pond'. He then tries to catch a frog. Frogs need not move until the catcher is near them because, of course, he will *hear* the jump – the 'ripple' in the still pond! When his emergency movement ration is used up, the frog must freeze. Any frog who feels relatively safe may rescue another in distress by using a move to create a diversion.

If space is limited, work with 3 or 4 frogs, with the rest of the class sitting to form the perimeter of the pond. Change catcher and frogs for each game.

Murder on the move Start with roughly one 'murderer' per five children! Murderers kill by touching victim between shoulder blades. No hitting or pushing!

Stand in a space. All close eyes. Touch your murderers. Murderers open eyes. Everyone else moves slowly around the room, eyes closed. Murderers work as a team and decide by silent mutual consent which one will kill first. When touched between the shoulders, victim screams and falls 'dead'. Everyone freezes and opens eyes. In the split second between touch and scream, the murderer must move into a position where he is not likely to be suspected. Ask for an accusation. If one of the murderers is accused he must sit out, whether he did the job or not! The victim sits out as well. The game continues until there are no more murderers or victims.

The 'dead' and 'condemned' who sit and watch get just as much fun out of this game as the active participants.

A series of variations and progressions on the basic exercise of listening to footsteps, followed by an exploration of walking and footstep patterns, creating an awareness of sound texture, rhythm and onomatopoeia.

1 Listening to footsteps

(a) Sit in a space, eyes closed. Follow the progress of one person around the room. *Point* at him as he moves around you, but do not move or make a sound. Begin with the teacher moving. Then let children take the lead as they understand the exercise.

(b) This time, don't point, but *raise your hand* when the person walks near you.

(c) Sit in a space, eyes closed, and listen as one person (A) moves amongst you. A touches someone else (B) who opens eyes and continues in his place. B touches a third person (C) who takes his place, and so on. How many *changes* were made?

(d) Eyes closed, listen to one person as he moves amongst you. Try to *remember his journey*. Eyes open. Discuss in pairs, and demonstrate to confirm. Start with simple movement patterns. Progress to the more complicated.

(e) Eyes closed. Listen to one person as he moves amongst you and silently *count his footsteps*. Begin again. This time, the person who has been moving *counts aloud but stands still*. Hands up as you think he would be passing you if he were following the same journey as before.

(f) Work as for (e), but use *handclap or tambour* to beat footsteps to represent the repeated journey. Pause several times and ask 'Where is he now?'.

(g) All eyes closed. Touch one child who opens eyes and weaves in and out of a group before returning to his place. Eyes open. *Who* was it?

(h) Choose *two* people (A and B) to start at opposite sides of the room. Half the class, eyes closed, points to A. The other half, eyes closed, follows the progress of B. A and B deliberately move alongside each other and cross pathways. Eyes open. Are you still pointing to the right person?

(i) Eyes closed. Touch a number of children who open eyes and stand up. They begin to move in unison, trying to put their feet down at the same moment. After a while, by silent mutual consent, they sit down again. *How many* people were moving?

A traditional listening game given an imaginative setting to form the basis for improvisation

Grandmother's footsteps (leading to Secret agents sequences) Grandmother stands at one end of the room, facing the wall. The children creep up on her, and freeze when she turns round. If she sees anyone moving, he must go back to the start line.

Give this well-known game a dramatic setting:

Work in small groups, escaping in the dead of night. Set out the journey with chairs and rostra blocks to indicate tunnels, passages, rivers, etc. Black out the room as much as possible. Replace 'grandmother' with a spotlight or cymbal. Let the light play over the room from time to time. Anyone caught in the light must freeze. Or, if a spotlight isn't readily available, use a cymbal roll. At the cymbal everyone is still and silent until the final reverberations have died away.

Secret Agents Enlarge this sequence by describing in detail the layout of a top-secret establishment – booby-trapped forests, mined swamps, walls 10 metres high, moats with trained guard sharks, intricate mazes, tunnels of poison gas, rooms without doors, etc.

In small groups, children discuss how they are to neutralise the reactor housed in the central chamber without waking any of the guards! They may use the most advanced equipment and have in their groups the cleverest inventors in the country.

However, they cannot tamper with the sound-alarm system which picks up *all* sound in and around the establishment, magnifies it to audible volume, and relays it to the guard house. This fool-proof system means there are no guards on patrol.

Groups must leave no evidence or bodies behind.

After thorough planning, let each group set any obstacles or structures they require for the journey. Obviously, many features will be shared by several groups, but it's easier to start in different areas. Use the whole hall and any adjoining areas. The larger and more interesting the space, the better.

Start from stillness and silence and use light and/or cymbal as control, as before.

Contrive that all groups finish at more or less the same time by setting a time limit. When all groups are on the return journey, state, 'You have five minutes to return to base,' and count down the final seconds to finish.

On return, call a general meeting so that each group can report to the others how they fared and how they tackled the problems.

This sequence engenders considerable excitement and group commitment and is a valuable language stimulus, motivating inventive problem-solving in the planning stage and colourful description in the talk-back.

Encourage groups to make up their own top-secret buildings, draw their own plans, and set other groups the task of penetrating their defences.

To complicate the issue you could set an unknown 'mole' in each group who is trying to sabotage the operation!

2 Different ways of walking

Practise walking as quietly as possible, as noisily as possible, wearing
shoes that hurt, wearing shoes that are too big, carrying a heavy
suitcase, with a limp, avoiding treading on the cracks in the pavement,
on stepping stones, along the corridor of a moving train, on a narrow
slippery bridge, on a tight-rope, as a child of three, as an old man.
(See Instant reactions, p. 65; Touch and die, p. 114.)
Encourage use of vocal sound to complement the footsteps. Listen to
the different sound patterns created during this exercise.
Talk the class through a walking sequence, e.g. Asleep in bed – wake
up – pull on some clothes – creep downstairs – open the door –
immediately you're in the middle of countryside you've never seen before
– turn to shut the door – door has disappeared – suddenly it's misty and
very cold – wade through the long wet grass in the field in front of you –
getting muddy underfoot – very squelchy – over the slippery tree trunk
laid across the stream – scramble up the slope – drier ground now –
getting warmer – mist is lifting – springy turf – prickly gorse – crawl
under the wire fence – on to the sand dunes – sink in the hot soft sand – on
towards the sea – sand firmer – sharp shingle – test the water – wade in –
lie on the water – feel the sun on your face – eyes closed – let the water
support you – and float ... – alarm clock rings – wake up – what are you
doing lying on the floor downstairs?
Or ask the group to *retrace* their footsteps. Having experienced the
'journey' they'll be able to remember a surprisingly long sequence.
One group can prepare a 'walking sequence' (dream, science fiction or
reality) and talk the rest of the class through it next lesson.

3 Moods

(a) **Altogether**   Walk as if you are sad, bored, resentful, impatient, in a
hurry, carefree, tired, bewildered. Discuss nuances of meaning.

(b) **Indian file**   Develop as an Indian file sequence. First person
chooses a 'mood' or is shown a flash card. He starts walking. The others
follow and copy, aiming to deduce what mood they are all in.

(c) **Groups**   Sit in groups and choose an adverb to describe the way you
will do a certain job – reluctantly, enthusiastically, clumsily, deftly, etc.,
and a job that you will ask another group to do – scrubbing the floor,
pruning the rose trees, rowing a boat, painting the Eiffel Tower. Now
make one large circle. Ask one group to start by naming the job to be
done. Another group moves into the circle and does that job according to
their chosen adverb. The others guess what the adverb is.

Footstep stories

(a) Ask the children to bring *different footwear* – wellingtons, flip-flops, football boots, diving flippers, etc. Listen to the different sounds they make. Make a 'sound-play' where the characters can be identified by the shoes they are wearing and the way they walk. Groups could present the plays to each other behind a screen.

(b) Take a tape recorder and record footsteps on *different surfaces*. Listen to sound-effect records of footsteps. Consider the onomatopoeic quality of words such as crunch, pad, squelch.

(c) Make sound effects with percussion and other objects to represent footsteps – an army marching, a horse trotting, a lady in high heels with a toy poodle walking beside her, a man with a wooden leg.

(d) Make up footstep 'music' using onomatopoeic words, sounds and percussion, and recorded effects. Good titles are: Carnival, Circus Parade, Creatures of the Moon, Walk on the Prom, Dog Show, The Lost World.

'I do know him by his gait' *Julius Caesar* Act I, scene 3.   Some people have distinctive walks and footsteps. Children can recognise teachers outside in the corridor, dogs know their masters' footsteps, horror movies often use distinctive footsteps to good effect. Discuss in small groups and create a short planned improvisation on the theme 'I do know him by his gait'.

Blind Captain Cat knew all the women of Milk Wood by their footsteps:

> All the women are out this morning, in the sun. You can tell it's Spring. There goes Mrs Cherry, you can tell her by her trotters, off she trots new as a daisy. Who's that talking by the pump? Mrs Floyd and Boyo, talking flatfish. What can you talk about flatfish? That's Mrs Dai Bread One, waltzing up the street like a jelly, every time she shakes it's slap slap slap. Who's that? Mrs Butcher Beynon with her pet black cat, it follows her everywhere, miaow and all. There goes Mrs Twenty-Three, important, the sun gets up and goes down in her dewlap, when she shuts her eyes, it's night. High heels now, in the morning too, Mrs Rose Cottage's eldest Mae, seventeen and never been kissed ho ho, going young and milking under my window to the field with the nannygoats, she reminds me all the way. Can't hear what the women are gabbling round the pump. Same as ever. Who's having a baby, who blacked whose eye, seen Polly Garter giving her belly an airing, there should be a law, seen Mrs Beynon's new mauve jumper, it's her old grey jumper dyed, who's dead, who's dying, there's a lovely day, oh the cost of soapflakes! Ocky Milkman on his round. I will say this, his milk's as fresh as the dew. Half dew it is. Snuffle on, Ocky, watering the town .... Somebody's coming. Now the voices round the pump can see somebody coming. Hush, there's a hush! You can tell by the noise of the hush, it's Polly Garter.

> Dylan Thomas *Under Milk Wood*

4 | Words

(a) **How many words?** Consider the number of verbs we have to describe walking or running. Work in groups and see how many you can think of.

(b) **Slow or fast verbs** In groups, choose 'slow verbs' or 'fast verbs' and make a list arranged according to speed of movement.
Here are a few suggestions (not arranged in order!):
Slow: slink, creep, crawl, slouch, shamble, waddle, toddle, hobble, plod, trudge, dawdle, saunter, totter, stagger, mince, shuffle
Fast: sprint, jog, trot, gallop, scuttle, scurry, scamper, dart, march, flit, swoop, dash, scoot

(c) **The right word** Consider the slight difference in emphasis between words of similar meaning. When would it be apt to use one rather than the other? Choose a number of walking/running verbs and use each one as 'the right word at the right time' in a story. Other members of the group illustrate the peculiar inference of the words by acting out the story as it is told.

5 | Walking in rhythm

(a) Start by walking to music. Use different tempi and time-beats. Experiment to see how many footstep patterns you can find to fit the same time-beat.

(b) Now, select one time-beat. Individually, practise a repeated pattern to fit it. Join a partner and teach him what you have been doing. Link your two sequences and practise together. Join another pair to make a four, and combine all four patterns into a sequence.

(c) Work without music, as for follow-the-leader. The first person claps or beats a rhythm and moves forward to it. The others copy and follow. Call 'Change!' The leader moves to the back of the line and the next person takes over with a fresh rhythm.

(d) Work in groups of five or six to develop (c) as a planned ritual dance. Try a rain dance, a war dance, a dance to bring good fortune or to ward off evil spirits.
(See also Stepping patterns, p. 21.)

Games

Call signs   Sit with a partner and think of a simple, short, individual call sign that both of you can make and recognise (a consonant said in a certain way, an intake of breath, a click of the tongue). Practise making your call. Now continue the lesson and contrive that partners are separated. Near the end of the lesson, eyes closed and original partners must find each other by making their call. To avoid a cacophony of sound, specify that each partner may make the sound only a limited number of times. As partners find each other they open eyes and sit silently.

Blind man's cry!   Stand in a circle. Choose a 'blind man' to stand in the centre. He points to someone in the circle and calls as if selling wares in the street, 'Fresh eggs for sale!' The person he is pointing to must echo the cry. If the blind man can guess (one try only!) whose voice it is, they change places.

Adam and Eve and the Serpent   Sit in a circle. Adam stands in the centre and closes his eyes. Eve is chosen and stands in circle. Adam says, 'Eve, where art thou?' Eve answers, 'I am here, Adam.' Adam tries to touch her. If he fails, he asks his question again. Eve may reply herself or may point to a Serpent who remains seated in the circle but replies instead of Eve. The same serpent may be used up to five times.

A letter a foot!   Choose a 'master'. The rest of the class stands side by side in a line in the middle of the room in front of the master. Master calls a letter. Each player must take as many steps *away* from the master as the letter occurs in his name. If it doesn't occur, the player may take one step forward. If the master repeats a letter, the whole class moves forward 3 steps. A 'step' is just one foot length, heel to toe! The winner is the first to get level with the master.

Exercises and games to illustrate different qualities of sound and encourage discerning listening skills.

Avoid competition in the exercises. A competitive atmosphere is not conducive to relaxed, receptive listening.

1 Using taped sound and percussion instruments

(a) Take three or four percussion instruments. Play each one. (Choose a very short rhythm.) Children, with eyes closed, listen as teacher plays them in haphazard order. Children open eyes, confer in small groups, and say how many different instruments were played or how many times they heard a certain instrument.

Or choose three or four different objects to drop on the floor (metal/plastic/wood/wool). Children close eyes to listen and, after conferring in groups, say how many different objects were dropped.

(b) Make a short tape-recording of animal sounds/street sounds or anything that suits your purpose. Children close eyes to listen and say at the end, after conferring in groups, how many different sounds they heard.

(c) Make a recording and select one sound in particular that you want the children to identify, e.g. bird song with a number of cuckoo calls. Children listen and say how many times they heard the cuckoo. Don't tell them they're listening for the cuckoo before you play the tape.

(d) Compare recorded sound with the sound of the same object made on the spot.

(e) Choose three or four coins. Spin them and listen to the different sounds they make. Eyes closed. Spin one. Children then confer to decide which coin was used.

Children will quickly want to set up their own 'picking out sounds' games, using tape recorders and objects.

2 Sound trays

Make up a tray of 'sounds', e.g.
(i) different materials in tins or jars – peas/rice/paper clips/water/etc.
(ii) objects of different textures – wood/paper/metal/etc.
(iii) everyday objects that make sound – pair of scissors/bunch of keys/jar with screw top/etc.
(iv) percussion instruments.
Children listen to differences in sound and then, eyes closed, indentify which object is picked up. As children become more familiar with this game, make sounds on each tray increasingly similar.

Development

Story with sound effects made by the class   Practise chosen sound effects first. Tell the story, pausing for children to participate by adding the appropriate effect.
Conduct to indicate 'louder', 'softer', 'stop'. A useful ploy to control volume is to suggest that the sound is in the distance – 2 kilometres away – 8 kilometres away.
Children can write and tell their own stories for sound effects.
Good titles are:

Noah's Ark (building the ark – the animals – the first rain drops – the thunder – the storm – etc.)
The farmyard (animals wake with the cockerel ...)
The coming of spring (winter winds – then icicles begin to melt – drip into streams – hibernating animals wake up – lambs – cuckoo – bees)
Bonfire night (see Firework display, p. 74.)
The sweet factory (see Sweets, p. 75, 76)
The clock shop (see Factory noises, p. 135.)

As the class becomes used to the idea of adding sound effects sensitively you can incorporate more solo sounds, allocate various effects to different groups who make the sound whenever appropriate, and invite spontaneous dialogue.

3 **All at once**

(a) **Song collectors** Sit in a space. Choose four or five 'song collectors'. Everyone else decides on a song to sing (hymn, carol, popular song, nursery rhyme). At a signal everyone sings his song at the same time (this demands tremendous personal concentration!) and the song collectors walk amongst the group seeing how many different songs they can hear. Silence on the cymbal!

(b) **Chant battle** In groups, choose a 'song' – First World War songs, football cheer leaders' chants or advertising slogans work well. Or make up your own 'war chant' using clapping rhythms.

Each group learns its chant. Groups take up position round the outside of the room. Two, on opposite sides of the room, are going to change places chanting as they move. The aim is not to lose your own chant and, if possible, to throw your opponent's chant into disarray! Work with four groups crossing from corner to corner.

Before you start this sequence, you could remove three or four members of the group. Bring them back to observe the 'chant battle'. Can they pick out the individual chants?

It is also useful as an inhibition breaker, if you need spontaneous mass singing as in *Oh, What a Lovely War!*, *Zigger Zagger*, etc.

(c) **Which proverb?** Work in groups of six or eight. Each group chooses a proverb and allocates one word per member of the group. If necessary, two people can share a word, or a long proverb can be split so that each person has two words. At a signal from the group leader, everyone says his word at the same time. Can the listening groups say what the proverb was?

Drawing sound developed as a group activity

Making a record   Work in groups. Give each group a large piece of paper, preferably circular with a hole in the middle, and a crayon.

The group is to make a 'record' – each person taking it in turn to create a phrase which he 'sings' to the group as he draws it. This phrase is repeated and learnt by the group before the next one is added.

You'll end up with an illustrated soundtrack, e.g.

When the record is complete, the leader takes the role of conductor and rehearses his group to performance pitch!

Obviously, at this stage, you can hold a 'recital' of the pieces. Or *redistribute* the drawings so that each group has to make sense of someone else's record.

Try playing the records at the wrong speed!

When the idea of 'drawing sound' has been grasped, groups will draw elaborate soundtracks, in several parts, using colour, objects and onomato-poeic words to indicate specific effects.

Activities stimulating imaginative and inventive responses to making
and listening to sound.

1 Symbols

Start with a simple symbol and change its size to indicate graduation of
volume, e.g.

What does  sound like?

The composite class sound is the one you want, so all individual noises
within that sound are correct!

In that case, what does ⌒ ⌒ ⌒ ⌒ sound like?

What do other shapes sound like?

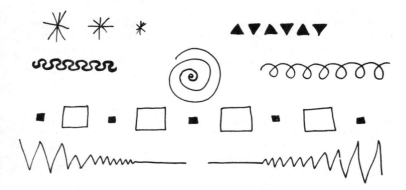

Indicate pitch by positioning shapes higher or lower:

Pace by spacing:

Tone by using different colours.

Making a tape Use a similar approach to make a tape, e.g.

If this is drawn on a roll of wallpaper it can be passed through the human 'tape recorder' that is to play it, re-rolled, and even played in reverse.

Take a pencil for a walk Take a pencil for a walk while listening to sounds or music.

Relax into the music and allow your hand to move spontaneously in sympathy with the tempo of the sound, creating shapes, patterns and pictures.

Sometimes it's interesting to compare your 'picture' with another motivated by the same sequence. Discuss the differences and similarities with your partner.

On a large floor area, use your body as the pencil and the floor as the paper. Make running, stepping patterns, change pace and pathways, make contact with the floor with different body parts – roll, spin, cartwheel – trace patterns with your feet or hands – whatever the sound dictates!

2 Body shapes

Make a shape with your body. What sound is the shape? A stretched, pointed shape would probably have a high, thin sound; a curled, ball shape might have a softer, rounder sound.

Work with a partner. Link your shapes and sounds into a 'singing-sculpture'.

Join another pair and create a larger sculpture. Continue until you have a composite class singing-sculpture.

Sounds may be made all at once, or in a pre-arranged or spontaneous order, or activated by onlookers' eyes as they walk round the sculpture.

(See also Sculpting, p 121; Group work on levels, p 129.)

3 Other things

Choose sounds to suit things.

Try an oak tree, a willow, a fir tree, a mirror, the moon, a sack of potatoes, a balloon, a lump of coal, an icicle, a cushion, a feather.

(See also Onomatopoeia, pp. 74–79.)

Sound and movement sequences sharpening reaction to chosen sound signals and developing critical and imaginative differentiation between various qualities of sound

(a) Finger puppets   Teacher makes a sound (percussion, vocal, hands). What could be making the sound? Children respond, and using hands only, like puppets, show *what* is making the sound. Add a second sound. What is it? Using the other hand, children show the perpetrator of that sound. What happens when the first 'sound' meets the second 'sound'?

(b) Puppet plays   Develop with small groups creating hand-puppet plays, each 'puppet' working to a theme sound. Set a rostra block or table on its side so that hands only can be seen.
   Work into more sophisticated sequences, making simple glove, stick or shadow puppets, and developing theme tunes for each character.

(c) Dance drama   Expand into dance drama sequences. Good titles are:

The money box (with each coin having its own theme tune based on its size, shape, value and the sound it makes when dropped)
Under the sea (a theme tune for the crab, the jelly-fish, the shark, the electric eel)
On safari (snakes, elephants, monkeys, gazelles)
most fables and fairy stories including, of course, *Peter and the Wolf.*

Whenever possible, work with live sound, allowing musicians and dancers to respond to each other, within a loose framework.

Stories using signals   Plan a group improvisation which involves receiving and communicating with signals.

Try: The curse of the pyramids
      Pot-holing adventure
      Bermuda Triangle
      The UFO
      The diving bell.

   You may need to use the international distress call – MAYDAY – or SOS (de-de-de dah-dah-dah de-de-de).

Exercises in giving and responding quickly to set sound signals and instructions.

---

1 **Controlling with sound**

(a) **Percussion** Choose 3 or 4 percussion instruments to 'control' movement, e.g. triangle means 'hop', cymbal means 'stop', drum means 'sit' tambourine means 'run'. Class responds to sounds.

(b) **Calling a partner** Work with a partner. A and B. Each pair decides on one sound, a call sign. Use percussion, claps or vocal sound. A's move to one side of the room, B's to the other. A's close eyes. Teacher points to people in the B group in turn. Each makes his sound and the corresponding A moves forward as the sound is made.
  (See Call signs, p. 54.)

---

2 **Controlling with code**

Work with a partner. A and B.
  Agree on four code words to stand for 'Move', 'Stop', 'Turn right', 'Turn left', e.g. 'Marmalade' could be code for 'Move'; 'Toast' for 'Stop'; etc. A is the controller, B the 'robot'. Practise using your code. Change over from time to time.
  B's close eyes. A stays close to B and guides him round the room whispering the secret code so that no one else can hear. Change over.
  When the codes are learnt, set up a competition! A's stand in a line along one side of the room, B's stand against the opposite wall facing their partners. Choose a pair to start. A closes eyes. Quietly place a sheet of paper on the floor between the two groups. Can A stand his robot on it, using the code words only? Tear the paper in half to make each successive attempt more difficult!

---

3 **Sound signals (into Aircraft landing)**

Work with a partner. A and B. Learn the following signals:
  a repeated steady note (Morse code O) dah-dah-dah dah-dah-dah
    means 'On course'
  a staccato note (S) de-de-de de-de-de
    means 'you're veering to the right (Starboard)'
  a broken rhythm (P) de-dah-dah-de de-dah-dah-de
    means 'you're veering to the left (Port)'

Games using signals

Minefield   The object of this game is for a controller to guide his 'blind' partner through the minefield without blowing him up!

Sit in pairs and agree on a number of sound signals (use Controlling with code, p. 63 or Sound signals, p. 63). Practise your codes.

Choose the first traveller who is to cross the minefield. He stands at one side of the room, eyes closed. His controller stands beside him. The rest of the class position themselves as 'mines' around the room. 'Mines' stand perfectly still. They may not reach for their victim but, if he touches them, they immediately grab hold of him and 'explode'. The 'blind traveller' starts his journey guided by his controller's signals. Will he cross the minefield safely?

Work with several travellers, each guided by his own controller, crossing at the same time.

Sheep dog trials   Adapt Controlling with sound, and ask each master to 'train' a 'sheep dog'. Arrange a number of 'pens' and set a course which the dogs must complete. Have a panel of judges who award marks for efficiency and deduct penalty points for sloppy handling!

Dog show   Work a similar sequence, asking each master to teach his dog (or dogs) an obedience routine or set of tricks. Watch one handler put his dog through its paces, and then ask a member of the 'audience' to take over. Of course, the dog will only respond to the commands it has been taught!

Robot shop   Various robots can be demonstrated for prospective customers. Improvise to develop a story.

(See Puppets, pp. 138–41.)

A is aircraft pilot. B is air traffic control. B's job is to guide A into a landing strip (a piece of newspaper).

A closes his eyes and moves off slowly (flying in thick fog!). If he hears a steady note he knows he is on course. As soon as the steady note is broken he knows that he is moving off course and must adjust accordingly.

Change over pilots and controllers. Also work with one aircraft and three controllers – each responsible for one signal.

When controllers and pilots are reasonably proficient, try a parachute drop! Aircraft pilot carries a handkerchief (the parachute) which must be dropped on target. Aircraft pilot closes eyes and the target (a chalk circle) is drawn on the floor.

The signal for 'Drop' could be 'dah-de-de' (Morse code D). Or use a firm handclap. After the drop, the pilot could open his eyes and, if it is a good landing, give the accepted signal for 'on target' (KK) 'dah-de-dah dah-de-dah'!

Work with several planes flying at once. In which case, you'll probably need a code name for each aircraft!

Encourage the class to develop the sequence with more signals and two-way communication between pilot and controller.

4 Following instructions

Work with a partner. A and B.

(a) Give A a picture of a person *doing* something. A instructs B to take up the same position as the person in the picture. A must not demonstrate, touch B or show him the picture until they have finished. How close is the copy to the original? Change over.

(b) A gives B step-by-step instructions to do a simple task. B does exactly as A tells him. How well is the job done? Change over.

(c) Work in small groups on a more complicated job. Instructions should be given by one or two members of the group who should have some expertise in the chosen task. They should take the task step-by-step and must not demonstrate or elucidate their original exposition. Think of them as being a 'speaking maintenance manual' or the recorded voice of 'Dial a Recipe', etc. Presume that the people doing the job are intelligent novices able to interpret the instructions with some common sense.

Discuss the problems, and agree on a clear, logical set of instructions.

5 Instant reactions

React to the instruction immediately. Give 'Freeze' signal between changes.

Games practising fast physical response

Versions of Simon says... The group reacts *only* if order is preceded by '*Simon* says', '*Big Brother* says', or whatever you choose.

Versions of fruit salad Sit on chairs in a circle. Choose four fruits – Apple, Pear, Peach, Plum – and label round the circle. Decide who is to begin and take away his chair. He stands in the centre of the circle and calls, '*Apples* – Change!' In which case, all *apples* change chairs, and the caller aims to sit in one of the empty chairs during the change-over. The person without a chair is the next caller. Of course, 'Fruit Salad' means that everyone must change chairs.

Try with names of stations (All Change!), countries (Round the World!). Use numbers, and let the caller add an instruction to the 'change!' command – 'Twos change *hopping*', 'Threes and Fours change *like mice*', 'All change *humming*', etc.

Trains Work with whole class or groups of 6 or 8. Stand in a line behind each other. Stretch arms out in front of you so that finger tips are about 10 cm from the shoulders of the person in front. Start 'shunting' forward. At a sudden signal 'train' must stop without any of the 'coaches' bumping into one another. After each 'stop', the leader goes to the back of the line. You can score by giving a penalty point to anyone who touches the person in front of him. The team with the lowest score wins!

Before the 'competition', trains can practise by taking the command from the one at the rear.

(a) **Walks**   Imagine you're on your way to a football match, to a funeral, walking on ice, on hot metal, on air, etc.
(See also Different ways of walking, p. 51.)

(b) **Escaping**   You're escaping from quicksand, from a room with one tiny window, from being tied up in a sack, through a tunnel, etc.

(c) **Dying**   You're machine-gunned, poisoned, strangled, stabbed in the back, dying from hunger, dying from thirst, etc.

(d) **Handicaps**   Fry an egg, tie your shoelaces, make a bed, bath the dog with your right arm in a sling.
Peel an orange, thread a needle, write a letter, do your hair without using your thumbs.
Sweep the floor, carry a bucket of water hopping on one leg.
Mix the disabilities, changing levels, and contrasting movement.
Use slow or fast motion and Changing weight and size, p. 149.

(e) **Statues**   Freeze as a statue representing pain, pleasure, fear, hatred, triumph, loss, loathing, alarm, shame.
(For further ideas, see section on Statues, pp. 124–31.)

Developments

Atmospheric chants   Use repeated vowel sounds, sung or chanted in a strange and solemn manner, as a processional chant in ritual sequences, e.g. to build mood and involvement before a sacrifice, rain dance, initiation ceremony, etc.

Let a number of 'high priests' process slowly to lead the ritual chant. Each sings a note which is echoed by the entire assembly. Aim to use a low hum to precede the main ceremony of the ritual. This can grow in intensity and change key at a strong simple gesture from the high priest. Cut the hum with a harsh gasp or bloodcurdling cry!

Experiment with other sounds and copied sequences.

(See Sound patterns and rounds, p. 91.)

Tape recorder games   Using a reel-to-reel machine, record one word several times ('barbecue' is a good one to start with). Now reverse the tape. On most machines this can be done by changing over the reels and twisting the tape. Listen to the word played in reverse. Copy it. Record the 'reversed word'. Now reverse the tape again. You should end up with the word you started with!

In small groups, work out a short sequence with simple dialogue and positive movement (melodrama sequences work well). Record the sequence. Reverse the tape. Learn the words in reverse and play your scene as if the film is running backwards!

Also use tape-recorded scenes played back at various speeds. Again melodramatic scenes work best.

Exercises to develop listening, copying and memory skill.

1 Copy this!

Sit in a space. Eyes closed.

(a) Teacher makes a sound (hand clap, finger clicks, stamp, vocal sound, etc.). Everyone copies, making the sound as they *think* it was made.

(b) Teacher claps a short rhythm. Class repeats it. Teacher adds a further phrase. Class repeats. And so on until you achieve as long a rhythmic sequence as is feasible.

2 Repeated sound circles

Sit in a circle.

(a) **Consonants** Each person thinks of a consonant and chooses a distinctive way of saying it (a smooth, long note/a short staccato rhythm). First person says his consonant. Everyone copies exactly. Second person continues with his sound. Everyone copies. And so on round the circle.
Avoid long pauses between different sounds. Aim for a following and pleasing pattern of sound.

(b) **Vowels** Work as for (a), but choose a long open vowel sound to sing or chant. Again, each sound is 'echoed' by the rest of the class.

(c) **Throwing sound** One person thinks of a sound which he 'throws' to another member of the circle. That person 'picks it up', repeats it, and 'throws' it to someone else.
(See also Throwing faces, p. 23; Eye contact circle, p. 27.)
When 'throwing sound', *record* the first and last sounds. Listen to the difference!

3 Echo valley

Work with a partner. A and B. Agree on a word, phrase or sound. Now leave your partner and lie down on the floor as far away from each other as possible. Eyes closed. A's are voices, B's echoes. Any A may begin by calling his sound which is echoed by his partner. Each 'echo' must listen carefully for his own 'voice' and, as there is no set order of speaking, timing skills are introduced as well.

Memory training games

I went to market and I bought . . .   Standard circle game, with each person repeating the shopping list and adding another item. For variation use 'I went to the circus and I saw . . .', 'I looked in the larder and I saw . . .' (any foods you care to mention!). In this sequence, encourage flavouring of words to indicate pleasant or unpleasant. The inflections should be kept and repeated as the list grows.

Detective game   Start by working in small groups with two detectives. Sit in a circle. The detectives state the crime, e.g. 'We're investigating a robbery which took place at the jeweller's in East Street between 9 and 10 p.m. last night.' They take it in turn to question the other people in the group, e.g. 'Where were you between 9 and 10 last night?' If that person answers, 'At home, watching television,' that fact must now apply to *everyone* in the group. The other detective might continue, 'Your car was seen in East Street. What is the registration number?' The person he points to answers, 'ABX 95T'. If later in the game he asks someone else, 'What did you say your car number was?' *that* is the number that must be given!

Detectives should ask questions briskly, sharing them between all voices of the suspect. Suspect is wise to answer briefly and simply!

The first suspect to be caught out is the guilty one!

Once the game is learnt, play in larger groups with several detectives.

4 Hired man

Work with a partner. A and B.

A decides on the job of work he is offering to do, and his particular skills and attributes, e.g. gardener/strong/honest/prize onion grower. He now has to 'sell' himself to B, and may have to add a few more details as B questions him. At a given signall *all* B's 'buy' their partners.

Each B now takes his 'hired man' to meet another pair. B repeats the information about A and adds a little embroidery of his own to make his 'hired man' more desirable/saleable. His object is to make the other master envious! B's assess the virtues of their 'hired man' and can agree to swap. The sequence continues with each new master augmenting and exaggerating his hired hand's attributes. Finally the 'hired men' can tell the class of the many talents they have acquired during the session!

5 Interminable conversation

Work with a partner. A and B.

(a) A starts, 'Did I tell you about that house?' (or whatever he chooses). B repeats the essential information 'House?' A feeds in more detail. Again B repeats, recapping the facts.

So the conversation might begin:

A Did I tell you about that house?
B House?
A Down by the canal.
B The house down by the canal?
A It's up for sale.
B The house by the canal is up for sale?
A Yes. The Baxters used to live there.
B So the Baxters' house by the canal is up for sale...

(b) With a more experienced group let each partner add to the initial statement as well as recapping.

Note that the object of this game is *not* to make an 'I went to the market' type list, but rather to develop listening and conversation skills by using an 'echo technique' to indicate understanding and invite further conversation.

6 Remembering tricks

(a) **Peg words and rhymes**   Sit in groups and chat about devices you each use to remember things. Perhaps you make up 'peg' words or sentences with the initial letters of the things you want to remember. Or you may use memory rhymes.

'Many a slip' game   Read a passage at the beginning of the lesson. Read it again at the end, with variations. Class must spot the differences! If you wish, play 'Many a slip' as a team game with points for correct challenges, etc.

A typical passage might read:

Jane and Andrew are second years at St Thomas's School, Hove.
   (Andrea)   (in the first year)   (Bartholomew's)

Jane walks to school every day but Andrew always takes the bus.
   (takes her bike)   (train)

Next week Jane is going on a trip to France with the school.
   (term)   (Paris)   (her family)

Andrew isn't going. He's playing for the school in the 1st eleven against
(Andrew's going too)   (for the county)   (2nd)

Downsbrook Comp. Last time St Thomas's lost, but Andrew wasn't in the
(Downswater Poly.)   (won)

team then!

Find some examples of these memory aids.

(b) **Names and numbers**   Do you have trouble remembering people's names? How do you cope with car and telephone numbers? Share your 'tricks' with the rest of the class!

(c) **Dramatic method**   You may already use dramatic method (making associations or stories) to help you remember things. For instance, if a person's name is 'Fred Parsons' you might think of Frederick the Great wearing a dog collar! and thus fix the name in your head! Find an association for all the names in your group!

To remember a list, create a story sequence incorporating all the items. Work round the groups compiling a 'shopping list' (10–20 items to start with). Write them down on the board, or have a scribe in each group. Now, quickly, each group must think of a story line to link each item. In a few minutes they should be able to recall all the items while mentally retelling the story! Try with an even longer list.

Developments

Drawing words   'Draw' words in such a way that the meaning becomes obvious, e.g.

Try – drip, crack, squash, squeeze, stretch, fluff, splash, sponge, sprinkle, gush, crag, crystal, shiver, crumble, whisk, twist, ooze, dribble, topple, bounce, swirl.

Firework display   In groups, make the sounds and use the onomatopoeic words associated with a particular firework, e.g. for a rocket you might have the fizz of ignition, the whoosh of ascent, the explosions, the cries of delight, the disappointment when it's over.

Use other well-known fireworks. Can we work out what they are just by listening to the sounds?

Add movement and create a *new* firework. Let another group think of a good name for it.

Sequences stressing the onomatopoeic aspect of language to further enjoyment in the 'flavour' and 'picture-painting' quality of words.

1 Sounds

(a) **Animals** What words do we use to describe the noises made by a snake, a hen, a duck, an owl, a bee, a dog, a frog, a lamb, a lion, a mouse, a pigeon, a rook, a pig, a wolf, a turkey, a donkey, a cat?

Consider both the words we use in imitation of the sound and the verb(s) one would normally use, e.g. dog: woof-woof/bow-wow/bark/grrrr/growl/howl.

(b) **Things** What words do we use to describe the sound of a stone dropped into water, a twig snapping in two, a clock, a cork coming out of a bottle, an explosion, horses' hoofs, brakes suddenly applied, light rain falling, leaves brushing against each other in the wind, glass breaking, a rubber band being stretched and released, a propeller turning?

Speak these words in such a way that there can be no doubt about what they mean!

2 Other words

Notice how texture, temperature, shape and size, taste, qualities of movement are expressed by words that sound right! For instance, take 'knife', 'fork' and 'spoon'. Think about the way you use each utensil and say the words. There is no doubt about which one is rounded, which one is sharp, which is pronged! 'Velvet' is a soft, furry word, whereas 'treacle' has to be sticky! An 'icicle' is cold and wet. 'Grit' is sharp and dry.

In groups, make your own lists of 'words that sound right'.

3 Sweets

Work in small groups. Think of the names of some sweets. Flavour and feel them as you say the name! Try chewing gum (a mouth exercise in itself!), fudge, acid drops, jelly lumps, liquorice, peppermint cream, lollipop, chocolate flake, bubble gum, salt and vinegar crisps.

Notice how clever many commercial names are. Choose some sweets that you think are well named. What about Twix, Kit Kat, Caramac, Chewits, Crunchie, Smarties?

Sweets

What is it called?   Working in groups, choose a name for your new sweet.
(See Sweets, on p. 75.)

What is it like?   What flavour, texture, colour, size, shape, wrapping, price
does the name suggest? And what makes your sweet special? Is it less
fattening, good for the teeth, more nourishing, relaxing, longer-lasting?

Television commercial   You have a thirty-second television commercial
spot to launch your sweet. Plan how you are going to use the time. What
visual impact do you want to make? Do you need a jingle or slogan, or a song
and dance routine? Who are you aiming the advertising at – children?
parents? gift-buyers? Remember, you have only thirty seconds to get your
message across – to sell your sweet.
   Prepare the 'commercials' for presentation using a proscenium arch acting
area. If you have a video camera, use it.
   Watch the commercials!
   Next lesson, ask for the *names* of the sweets again. Obviously, the group
that thought up each sweet should not answer!) See how much 'advertising
material' has been retained!

Local radio commercial   Prepare a thirty-second commercial for local radio.
Of course, everything you want to say must be contained in sound and words.
Choose or make any sound or music you need, and tape your commercials.
   Keep the tapes and play them in a natural break in a lesson later in the
term!

Sales talk   Mix groups and work in pairs. One is a shopkeeper. The other is a
salesman for his sweet firm. Convince the shopkeeper that your new sweet
will be a best-selling line. Shopkeepers are not going to waste display space
unless they are persuaded!

Vox pop   Choose one of the sweets. The firm is running a big advertising
campaign in the town centre on market day. All shoppers will be offered a
free sample – and asked for their opinion. Television cameras are there to
record the event!

Suppose a new sweet is being launched. It's called Cric-Crac. What does it look like, feel like? How is it packaged? Who do you think will buy it?

In your group, pass some Cric-Crac round and, as you say the name, begin to taste the sweet. Discuss and decide exactly what Cric-Crac is. Now try Chewsey, Scrumble, Lulus, Rufflettos.

4 Onomatopoeia in other languages

It's interesting to compare the following words used in imitation of sounds:

cockerel	cock-a-doodle-doo	(English)
	cocorico	(French)
	kikeriki	(German)
	chicchirichi	(Italian)
		(hard 'k' sounds as in the German)
hen	cluck-cluck	(English)
	cot-cot-cot-codette	(French)
	gack-gack	(German)
	coccode	(Italian)

Listen for examples of onomatopoeic words in other languages. Make your own collection. Here are a few to start:

French	*graveleux* (gritty)
	bouillon (bubble)
Italian	*schiamazzo* (din) – it even looks noisy!
	raschiamento (scraping/scratching)

5 Commentaries using 'Talking into hands'

(a) **Gibberish** Talking all at the same time, use gibberish to describe a graveyard at midnight, an exciting sporting event, a peaceful country scene.

Listen to the varying tone, pitch and pace of the class sound.

(b) **Talking into hands** With your hands cupped over your mouth, like a very close microphone, talk quietly, using *words* to describe the same scenes.

'Talking into hands' is a very useful stratagem to develop flow and confidence in speech. The barrier of hands in front of mouth gives a sense of security and privacy to the talker which favours experiment. The important thing is that there is no pressure. No one need hear, unless you want them to!

Onomatopoeic games

Verbs in use   Sit in a circle. First person starts, 'Listen, I'm *growling'* (spoken with all the onomatopoeic quality he can muster). The class repeats, 'Listen, he's growling!' And so on, with each person using a different verb – gurgling, choking, hissing, coughing, snoring, murmuring, yawning, sighing, whispering, etc.

I like/I hate   Sit in a circle. First person says 'I like ripe apricots' (or whatever he chooses) savouring and lingering over the delicious food as he speaks. Everyone copies his inflection and facial expression. Next person says 'I hate ripe apricots!' spitting the words out in disgust. Everyone copies. The third person starts with a new item, 'I like red jelly!' And so on round the circle. (Of course, you needn't stay with foods.) Also try starting with 'I hate ...'. The contradiction usually has greater intensity than the statement that precedes it.

I am a ...   Sit in a circle. Everyone thinks of a breed of dog. The first person starts, 'I am a bulldog', spoken in such a way that we know exactly what a bulldog is like – how big, how strong, how fierce, how proud, etc. The class copies his inflexion exactly and repeats, 'He is a bulldog!' The next person might choose, 'I am a Pekinese' (presumably a high little voice with a Chinese accent!). The class repeats, 'He/she is a Pekinese!' And so on.
  Try also makes of cars, foods, sweets, fireworks, weather.

Towns   Work in small groups. Choose a town – Slough, Chichester, Newport Pagnell. Groups must decide '*What* is a slough?' or '*How* do you chichester?' Each group comes up with a definition and illustrates it by using the word in a short scene.

(c) **Commentaries** Talking altogether, into your hands, give 'commentaries' on the room you're in. Or recall an everyday occurence or recent event – morning registration, the swimming gala. Capture the colours, shapes, sounds, smells, atmosphere to 'paint a picture' in words!

(d) **Running commentaries** Set up situations (or take advantage of suitable sequences as they arise naturally in lessons) – a carnival procession, a wedding, a race (run in slow motion), and let the other groups give commentaries (into hands) as they watch.

Working in groups, half the group could act out a situation – an investiture, an assassination, a sporting event (use slow motion) while the others give as vivid a commentary as possible.

'Act out' nursery rhymes or fairy stories. In this case, you might subdivide your group into three – actors, commentators and sound effects! Present these sequences, using the humour of acting and telling a well-known story for young children to wean from talking into hands to communicating with an audience.

Development

Zoo on Planet X   What animals might be in a zoo on Planet X? – creatures we have never seen, animals that are quite common on earth, even humans?
Working individually or in small groups, become an animal for the zoo. Think and react: How big are you? What colour? Covered in scales, fur, feathers, skin? How do you move – paws, flippers, wings, hoofs, etc.? What do you eat? What sound do you make? Explore sounds by suggesting motivation. Relax.
Now think about the inhabitants of Planet X. Ask for suggestions. Suppose the first person says, 'They're very tall.' Everyone gets up, stretches and walks tall. Another suggestion – 'They have tin legs and arms.' Movement becomes stiffer. Another suggestion – 'They blink a lot.' (Here it would be worth asking, 'I wonder why?' Is the light on Planet X very bright? Or has it become brighter suddenly? Or is blinking a mechanism to regenerate brain cells? Let the class tell you!)
When you have established Planet X and its inhabitants, add that they all talk in gibberish.
Chat with each other, in gibberish, about the shocking weather you're having and how it affects you, the earth rocket you saw the other day, the latest fashions, and the fact that you're all going to the zoo tomorrow.
Roughly one-third of the class will be visitors to the zoo. Two-thirds are animals in the zoo, with their keepers. Choose which you want to be.
Set up the zoo and open the gates to the visitors. Develop in spontaneous improvisation.
What would happen if that earth rocket landed in the middle of the zoo?

Sequences to draw attention to the emotional content of sound, and to stimulate vocal experiment and flexibility; followed by intonation exercises illustrating the diversity and subtlety of the spoken word, and developing range in pitch, pace and tone.

1 Animals

(a) **Favourite animals**   All together, make the noise of your favourite animal. Conduct – louder, softer, different sections, individual sounds and stop.

(b) **Animal choirs**   Think of the noises that other animals make – lions, snakes, horses, cows, chickens, dogs, cats, mice, bees. Divide into animal groups and organise yourselves as lion choirs, mouse choirs, etc. Choose a conductor for each group.

(c) **Motivation**   Now specify the motivation for the sound – hunger, anger, contentment. Listen to the subtle differences in sound in each group. Try angry wasps, lazy bees, frightened fieldmice, well-fed lions all together.
(Finish each sequence with a placid sound to 'de-climax' the group.)

(d) **Invented sounds**   Now stretch the imagination! What about indignant goldfish, snooty giraffes, harassed spiders, cheeky tadpoles, sleepy slugs?
Working in small groups, try tortoises telling funny stories, or ants complaining to each other, centipedes on their way to the chiropodist, worms singing lullabies, etc.

(e) **Invented creatures**   Draw a strange creature. What sound does he make? What sound does he make when he's frightened, happy, sleepy, etc.?
Use creatures drawn by the children. (See Fantastic animals, p. 132.)

(f) **And people** *(human animals!)*   What sound do you make if someone stands on your toe, if someone gives you a present, slaps cold rice pudding on your face, accuses you falsely, tells you an improbable story, points a gun at you?

(g) **Watching the television**   Imagine you are watching the television. By the sound of your reactions, show what is happening on the screen. Teacher may take the initiative and begin by laughing (that's funny!), yawning (boring!) drawing in breath (violent!), etc. Or, with a more experienced class, let the initiative pass freely within the group.

Further developments in improvisation

Interpreters   The scene is an international conference with guests from far-distant and little-known countries. Everyone speaks his own version of gibberish.

Working individually, everyone imagines that he is demonstrating how to prepare a popular dish from his country.

Take one of the demonstrators and assemble the other guests to listen to him. Introduce him formally, and also introduce the *one* person in the room who understands his language. He will interpret into English for the assembly, sentence by sentence, as the demonstration takes place. (This may seem a daunting task, but there isn't any great pressure on the interpreter who may say, within reason, whatever comes into his head!)

There is no conferring (except, if necessary, in their common gibberish tongue) between demonstrator and interpreter. The demonstrator and interpreter should not resist each other's ideas, but should work in sympathy with each other.

Work a similar sequence demonstrating national dress, a new invention, giving a weather report.

Many other sequences may be worked using gibberish, and calling in an interpreter as necessary.

Try: Buying and selling sequences
      Problems at Customs
      Sight-seeing
      Ordering a meal
      Hijack

2 Whistle talk

Work with a partner and aim to communicate messages in whistle, hum or groan talk!

How do you ask a question? How do you show that you disagree? What else can you deduce from the *inflexion* of the sound? Obviously eye contact, facial expression and gesture are also essential elements in this communication. Try working back to back to see how much you can pick up from inflexion alone.

3 Gibberish sequences

(It's not *what* you say, but the *way* that you say it!) Encourage use of gesture and body language in these exercises.

(a) **Alphabet language**   Using the letters of the alphabet as 'words', soothe a crying infant, complain on the telephone, explain how to wire up a plug, give someone a telling off, sell fruit in a street market.

(b) **Gibberish conversations**   Work with a partner and use alphabet language or 'gibberish' (any sound combinations or nonsense words you choose to convey your meaning) to argue, gossip, nag, wheedle, charm, inspire, ridicule, conspire, console.

(c) **Foreign tongues!**   Use 'gibberish' and talk in groups as if you are French, German, Italian, Russian, Chinese, stiff-upper-lip British, etc.

4 Inflexion circles

(Inflexion is the upward and downward glide of the voice on words and syllables that gives finer points of meaning and emphasis to speech.)

(a) **Yes/No**   Work round the circle, everyone saying 'Yes'. Each 'Yes' is repeated by the rest of the group. Discuss the numerous shades of meaning inferred by different inflexions. Repeat with 'No'. Consider the dictionary definition – 'Affirmative'/'Negative'. How far is the spoken word contained within those confines?

(b) **Intensity**   Take the word 'No', and pass it quickly round the circle, increasing the intensity of the word as each person says it, e.g. the first person isn't bothered, but the last person really means '*No!*'

Work in reverse from intense to uninterested.

Run a similar sequence with 'Yes'.

(c) **Other words**   How many ways can you say 'Sorry', 'Hello', 'Thank you', 'Look', 'Goodnight'? Listen to the inflexions and imagine what has provoked each response.

The unseen partner:
Telephone conversation
(a) Altogether, everyone answers a telephone. The only response that may be made is 'Yes', repeated as many times as required and inflected to give different meanings.

(b) Repeat, with just one person answering the phone. The others listen and imagine *who* is on the other end of the line.

(c) Limit the conversation to five or six responses. Practise together, then listen to one person answering the phone. Re-run the same telephone call. Can anyone supply the other side of the conversation?

Answering the door   Answer either 'Yes' or 'No' (as many times as you like) to an unseen person at the door. Who is it? What does he want?

Overheard   Try 'Oh' or 'Really', overheard from another room.
Use any of these ideas as starters for improvisation.

A song of sixpence

> *Sing a song of sixpence*
> *A pocketful of rye*
> *Four and twenty blackbirds*
> *Baked in a pie*

Use these words as the dialogue between a motorist and a traffic warden or policeman, a teacher and erring pupil, customs officer and traveller, salesman and customer, etc.

The lines must be spoken *in order* throughout the improvisation, e.g. if the traffic warden opens with 'Sing a song?' (inferring, 'This is your car?'), the motorist must respond 'Of sixpence!' (Yes, it is!). He may then continue 'A pocketful of rye four and twenty' ('I was just getting some change ...') etc. When they get to the end of the rhyme, they start at the beginning again!

Requiring the lines to be spoken in order demands a high degree of concentration and allows a feeling for the pattern of language to develop between partners.

One-word plays   Working in groups, take *one word,* e.g. 'custard' or 'hippopotamus', and repeat it with varying inflexions, tone, pitch, pace, volume and intensity to make the dialogue in your play!

(d) **Distance**   Choose a name, e.g. 'Richard'. The first persons says 'Richard' as if he is very close by, the second person calls slightly louder as if Richard is the other side of the room, the third person calls louder and longer, and so on, until finally we presume that Richard is miles away!

The secret is to *lengthen* the vowels, not to shout!

Try the old 'Jump Now!' sequence, working round the circle in pairs or fours:

Crowd watches a face at the first floor window – the building is on fire – they call 'Jump Now! – he goes up to the second floor – they shout louder – etc. – from the tenth floor he jumps – what sound do they make?

(e) **Message in a name**   Choose a name. Working round the circle, use the one name to convey a complete message, e.g. 'Richard' (meaning 'You shouldn't have brought me a present'), 'Richard' ('The chip pan's on fire!'), 'Richard' ('I'm warning you …')

---

5   **Reading in character and situation**

Read a passage (picked at random from a book or a pile of torn-up newspapers and magazines). Forget about what it actually says, and read it as if it is the following:

the News read without emotion
a bedtime story for a three-year-old
a sermon given by an elderly vicar!
an invective by a dictator
a secret message passed between spies
a scandalous news item
a political speech by a passionate extremist
a declaration of love
the climax of a revivalist meeting in the Southern States.

Break the passage with pauses so that it becomes:

a recipe
a shopping list
one side of a telephone conversation.

Practise *timing skills* by pretending that you're all old people in a club finding interesting items in your newspapers and waiting for your moment to butt in and deliver your piece of news/gossip to the others.

Develop *projection* and *enunciation* by requiring two people to read and be understood by each other over a gabble of other voices reading the papers.

Place the pair who are trying to communicate as far apart as possible, and make them project across rising wind and storm noises made by the rest of the group.

Games

Accents game   Sit in small circles. A, B, C, D and E. A says, 'I come from ...' (wherever he chooses, and with the dialect or accent to match). Everyone repeats 'He comes from ...'. A continues 'I come from ... and my name is ...'. Everyone repeats. A continues adding one more piece of pertinent information each time! After a time limit, or as memories fail, B takes over with a different accent.

Listen critically to the accents (preferably genuine ones). Consider the various qualities and tones they add to people's voices. Do they sound warm, sincere, aloof, glib, sad, cheeky, comic, serious, lazy? Does it make a difference if it's a man or a woman's voice? Feel how the mouth is shaped differently to make various regional vowel sounds.

Intonation game   Sit in small circles. How many different meanings can you draw from these sentences by changing stress, tone, pitch and pace?

I thought you were going home today.
You are not going to Susannah's house.
George gave Andrew five pounds.
I didn't know you could do that.

Neutralisation game   Work in pairs. Can you make sense of these sentences by varying the degrees of neutralisation on 'had' and 'that'?

If Jones had had had instead of having had had, he would have had a correct translation.

The phonetician said that that that that that student said in that way was not the that that he thought that he had said.

(Jones wrote 'had had' instead of 'had', and the student said 'that' differently to the way originally thought!)

Imagine you are reading in a vast echoing cathedral. Speak slowly with each word strongly enunciated and defined. The others provide the echo.

Finally, use as a *pace* exercise. Give a horse-race commentary with members of the group taking over from each other at different stages in the race. First one sets the scene – then they're off – over to the grandstand – and coming in to the final bend – the home stretch – the finish.

It may be helpful to note that newspaper is also used in Paper balls, p. 151 and Dexterity, p. 167.

6 Emphasis and neutralisation

(a) **Finding key words and subordinate words**
Speak a sentence stressing every word. You'll notice that the more words you emphasise, the less effective the emphasis becomes! Emphasis implies neutralisation – the surrendering of subordinate words.

Work in pairs and look at some passages. Find the key words that should be emphasised and the subordinate words that must be surrendered to make the emphasis effective.

O FOR A MUSE OF FIRE THAT WOULD ASCEND
THE BRIGHTEST HEAVEN OF INVENTION,
A KINGDOM FOR A STAGE, PRINCES TO ACT
AND MONARCHS TO BEHOLD THE SWELLING SCENE!

(b) **Pointing** Prepare a passage for reading aloud by underlining the important words and phrases – the words you wish to 'point'. For instance:

> When a bar <u>revolves</u> between <u>two blocks</u> – with no <u>lubricant</u> – surface <u>contact</u> causes <u>wear</u> and <u>heat</u> – a complete <u>waste of energy</u>. As the blocks <u>close</u> the surfaces <u>weld together</u>. This causes <u>more</u> waste. Parts <u>wear out</u> – and have to be <u>scrapped</u>. And the <u>culprit</u> is <u>friction</u>.

Remember, there are more ways of 'pointing' a word than simply increasing the volume! Use inflexion, and pause before the word you wish to emphasise.

(c) **The neutral vowel** Notice the use of the neutral vowel (the sound ə as at the end of moth*er*). In the following extract neutral vowels are written in small print.

Game

What are we watching? In groups, choose a television programme to 'watch'. other groups observe and listen to reactions and say *what* each group is watching. You'll find that groups can be quite specific in the choice of programme, and subtle and penetrating in their reactions, e.g. How much can you convey with a 'laugh' – a side-splitting joke, clever wit, gentle humour, cynicism, etc. Also, people in the group may react slightly differently, giving further clues as to the nature of the programme. Encourage an analytical approach in other groups, not random guessing!

I wandered lonely as a cloud
That floats on high o'er vales and hills
When all at once I saw a crowd,
a host of golden daffodils,
Beside the lake, beneath the trees
Fluttering and dancing in the breeze

Neutralisation controls meaning as well as flow. Take a simple sentence (with neutral vowels marked);

He was the leader of a youth group.

Consider the change of meaning if we lose some of the neutral vowels. Any weight on 'was', or 'the' or 'a' lends a different implication to the sentence.

Note that neutralisation does not imply inaudibility or lazy diction! Rather it requires greater strength and flexibility and is vital to the flow and rhythm of natural speech.

Developments

Musique concrète In groups, create rhythmic sound sequences on themes. Work as for Sound patterns – building a sound sequence, adding sounds, words and rhythmic phrases to suit the chosen theme.

Try Clock factory, Black magic, Strange machine.

Use the sound sequences as a stimulus for improvisation or movement. (See also Footstep stories, p. 52; Making machines, Abstract machines, Factory noises, pp. 134–6.)

Tempo and pace Choose a pace pattern for a scene, i.e. starts very slowly – suddenly speeds up – gradually slows down again. In groups, work out a story to fit the changes in pace, i.e. lazily fishing until you get a bite, struggle to land the fish, but he gets away. Many, many stories will fit the same pace pattern.

Now each group chooses its own pace pattern and works out a story. The pace patterns should be clapped before the scenes are presented. Discuss the effect of changes in pace on the audience.

Deliberately play a scene with a very even pace. Time the scene. Now consciously aim for contrasts in pace. Both scenes may take the same length of time but the second one is likely to be more pleasing.

Exercises to foster pleasure in rhythmic patterns and to develop an awareness of pace and tempo.

---

1 **Sound patterns**

(a) **Stop when I stop!**   Sit on the floor in a large circle so that everyone can see everyone else. One person starts to beat out a simple repeated rhythm of claps, using floor, hands and knees. The others copy, and stop when he stops.

(b) **Crescendo**   Work as for (a), but this time the leader builds to a climax. The others copy and build with him, and aim to stop when he stops.

(c) **De-climax**   Work as for (a), but go on to 'de-climax'. Slow down and become quieter together and finish in silence. Hold the silence at the end of this sequence.

(d) **Building a sound sequence**   One person starts by choosing a time beat which he beats out firmly. The next person adds a sound to fit in with the beat and amplify the rhythm. Continue round the circle and an intricate rhythmic sequence will develop.

(e) **Clapping rounds**   Work in groups of 4/8. Choose four patterns that fit the same time beat. Join the four patterns into a '4-bar' sequence and learn it. Work as for Rounds with the second person joining in after the first 'bar'.

---

2 **Rounds**

Work in a circle. The *second* person begins when the first person has finished the first line, the third person when the second person has finished the first line, and so on!

Use (i) Jelly on a plate
        Jelly on a plate
        Wibble wobble, wibble wobble
        Jelly on a plate

   (ii) Chop chop choppity chop
        Chop off the bottom and chop off the top
        What we have left we will pop in the pot
        Chop chop choppity chop

Rhythm games

Names and Ha-ha! are useful ice-breakers.

Clap, clap, click, click and Matthew, Mark, Luke and John are well-known concentration games practising imediate response.

Names Clap out the rhythm of someone's name – 'John Smith', 'Alexis Papadopoulos', 'David Cooper'. etc. Listen to the rhythm and say whose name it is.

Or use this game as a mixing exercise: Find a name-rhythm twin! (someone with the same name-rhythm as yourself). Continue together to see if you can group into quads! And so on, until the class is divided into name-rhythm groups.

Ha-ha! Sit in a circle. First person says 'Ha!'. Second person says 'Ha-ha!'. Third person says 'Ha-ha-ha!'. And so on round the circle.

Work quickly and notice how you tend to group the multiple 'Ha-has' into rhythms.

A hilarious development is to play this in a 'Ha-ha line'. Lie down in a zig-zag line, each person at right angles to the one in front and with his head on his tummy! Have two teams and see which can complete the Ha-ha line most efficiently!

Clap, clap, click, click Stand in a circle. Number round the circle. Practise the rhythm – clap, clap, click, click. The claps are 'thinking time'. You *speak* on the finger clicks. On the first click you say your own number, on the second click you call someone else's number. He must answer on *the next set of clicks* by repeating his number and calling someone else. If someone is late in response, he folds his arms but stays in the circle and everyone must remember that that number is 'out of action'. If an 'out of action' number is called by mistake, the caller goes 'out of action' too. Play briskly, with the number above the one last 'out' starting the next sequence immediately.

Use as an introduction to Matthew, Mark, Luke and John.

Matthew, Mark, Luke and John Sit on chairs in a circle. Name and number round the circle – Matthew, Mark, Luke, John, one, two, three, etc. Matthew is the leader and the object of the game is to sit in Matthew's chair. Make the point that you are numbering the *chairs* rather than the players! Matthew starts the beat, usually a steady clap, with a response expected on each beat. He claps and calls his own name followed by someone else's name or number, 'Matthew to nine'. If nine responds, say, 'Nine to John', all well and good. But if nine fails to respond he must vacate his chair. Number ten then moves into nine's place, and so on round the circle, leaving the chair furthest away from Matthew for the original number nine. Remind the players that they respond according to the chair they are sitting in, not the number they were first given!

(iii) Boiled potato
Mashed potato
Fried potato
Crisps!

Ask groups to make up their own rounds. Encourage variety of tone and pitch, and full flavouring of onomatopoeic words in 'presentation'.

---

3 Word trains

This menu train is well known, and serves perfectly to introduce the idea to a class.

Repeat each item the number of times indicated.

Coffee	× 6
Cheese and biscuits	× 5
Plums and custard	× 4
Beef and carrots	× 3
Fish and chips	× 2
Soup	× 1

Start very slowly, 'puffing steam' with 'coffee', then pull out of the station to 'Cheese and Biscuits', gather speed for the rest of the menu until the train disappears into a tunnel with a long whistle of 'Soup!'

Practise together so that the tempo of the piece is learnt. Then divide the class in half, to form two trains. One train starts at the station with 'Coffee'. The other is travelling in the opposite direction, leaving the tunnel at full speed with 'Soup!'. Listen to the rhythms as the trains 'pass' each other. Of course, they should both finish at the same time!

Work similar sequences with different menus. Place names also work well.

Try a rocket launch and space flight instead of a steam train journey!

---

4 Word rhythms

Think of words as either 'steady and balanced' or 'bumpy and about to fall over themselves'. In groups, agree on a collection of five of the best of each type.

What about train, strong, flavour, earth, arm chair, proverb, owl, wall as balanced words; polyanthus, statistician, hicupping, aluminium, inexplicably as bumpy words?

Compare and discuss each group's selection.

Word games

Choosy Jane Choose a vowel which 'Jane' doesn't like. Suppose Jane can't stand 'e's. What can we give her for her birthday? A pair of socks (but not shoes), a box of biscuits (but not a packet of sweets), a wild lion (not a tame elephant).

Play in small groups. With a younger group, choose a consonant. Jane can't stand 'd's. What can we give her for her birthday? A blue skirt (but not a red dress), etc.

Spare pairs Each player thinks of two rhyming words which can be guessed from a clue he also makes up. First person starts, 'I have a spare pair. It's a girl from Switzerland.' The answer is, of course, 'Swiss miss'! An angry employer is a 'cross boss', a thousand watt spot is a 'bright light', a careful scholar is a 'prudent student', a shy hooligan is a 'quieter rioter', and so on!

Play as a circle game with each person taking it in turn to set a 'spare pair', or as a team game with each team challenging the other in turn.

Coffee pot One person, or a small group, chooses a *verb* which the others must discover by asking questions. In the question and answer session, the chosen verb is always referred to as 'coffee-pot'; e.g. If the verb is 'to breathe', the conversation might run like this:

Q. Can you coffee-pot?
A. Yes! Everyone coffee-pots.
Q. How did you learn to coffee-pot?
A. I didn't have to learn. I just started coffee-potting.

Exercises and games to build vocabulary and tighten definition in speech.

1 Word chains

Sit in a circle.

(a) **Beginning and ending of letters** Each word must begin with the last letter of the previous word - TIN-NOW-WET-TOP-PIN. Each word should be spoken clearly with strong consonant sounds.

(b) **Categories** The first person chooses the category - say, 'Cars'. Continue round the circle, one 'car' each - 'Ford Escort'; 'Renault 5', etc. If a person cannot think of another car, he calls a fresh category - 'Breeds of dog'.

(c) **Alphabetical order** Describe a person, one adjective each, e.g. Jane is amusing, beautiful, clever, etc. Or pack a suitcase - I'm going on holiday so I shall pack an aqualung, a balalaika, a cardigan, etc. Any member of the group may challenge 'What for?', and the person who suggested the obscure item has to explain why he needs to take it on holiday with him! Play also as a memory game. See I went to market and I bought, p. 70.

(d) **Word flow** This is a word association exercise in which the sound and texture of the word come into play as well as the meaning: e.g. dash - flash - crash - crunch - munch - chew - shoe - whoo - tuwit tuwhoo - night owl - growl.

2 Mouth mobility

(a) Try to say each of the following six times, crisply and clearly, without tripping over your tongue!

Unique New York
Peggy Babcock
Mr Mick's Mixed Biscuits
Six thick thistle sticks
Good blood, bad blood
Red lorry, yellow lorry

(b) Pass the following pieces of 'gossip' round the circle. Start slowly and let the pace and excitement mount as the gossip is passed on.

Betty Blue blows big black bubbles
Freckled-faced Freda feasts on fresh figs
Lewis laid a long ladder lengthways on the lawn

Collective nouns Work in paired small groups. One group thinks of something that should be given a collective noun and challenges the other group – 'Tea bags!' for instance. They confer for a few seconds and come up with their suggestion, say – 'A *perforation* of tea bags!' It is now their turn to challenge – 'Light bulbs!' The other group thinks and offers 'A *switch* of light bulbs?' If the challenging group is unhappy with the suggestion they can reject it, giving reasons. In which case another collective noun must be found – 'A *shine* of light bulbs!'

Word tennis Stand opposite a partner and 'bat' words to each other. Use a 'theme' for each set – beginning and ending letters, categories, alphabetical order (as in word chains). Server chooses the theme. First person to falter loses the set! Play 'doubles' as well as 'singles'. Run a tournament.

Call My Bluff! Play in paired teams of 3. For each round each team chooses an uncommon word and thinks of three definitions for it – one true, two false. These can be written on cards and prepared by the teams in advance. Each team gives a list of the chosen words to the chairman who invites them to give their definitions. The opposing team must say which definition is the true one.

The trick is, of course, to speak fluently, with authority, and make all definitions equally plausible – or unlikely!

Richard's shop sells shot silk socks with spots on them
The thick thrush flew through the thorny thicket
Old oily Olly oils oily autos
The crow flew over the river with a lump of raw liver in his mouth
She stood on the balcony inexplicably mimicking him hicupping and
welcoming him in.

(c) Have a conversation with a partner in which every word is spoken
twice, e.g.

A It's it's cold cold in in here here.
B It it always always is is.

(d) Work a similar sequence inserting 'sir' between each word in the
sentence, e.g.

Please sir will sir you sir let sir me sir go sir!

3 Voicing

Working individually, put your hand on your throat and feel the
vibrations as you speak.

Say: 'p' (as in pin)   then   'b' (as in box)
        't' (as in tin)   then   'd' (as in dog)
        'c' (as in cat)   then   'g' (as in gate)

Each pair of sounds is made by contact, hold and explosive release of the
same organs, but the first sound is voiceless (no vibrations on the vocal
cords) while the second is voiced, and can be felt.

Try: 'f' (as in fan   then   'v' (as in van)
        'th' (as in think)   then   'th' (as in then)
        's' (as in sing)   then   'z' (as in zoom)

The same applies, but these sounds are 'fricatives' made by restricting
rather than blocking the flow of air. Feel the friction points used in the
making of each pair of sounds.
    The following interesting pair of sounds starts with a closure and then
becomes a fricative:

        'ch' (as in child)   and   'j' (as in judge)

Try the sounds 'm' (as in mother), 'n' (as in now) and 'ng' (as at the end of
song). In each case the mouth is completely closed at some point so the
sound must pass out through the nose. They are all voiced, so put one
hand on your throat, the other across your nose, and feel the vibrations!
    All vowel sounds are voiced, and there are 24 of them in the English
language, not counting the hundreds of regional variations!

Two concentration games using number

Cheese   Sit in a circle. First person starts 'One'. Second person 'Two'. And so on until the seventh person. 'Seven' is the forbidden word, which can only be referred to in hushed tones as 'cheese'.

So seven becomes 'cheese'
     seventeen   'cheese-teen'
     twenty seven   'twenty cheese'
     seventy   'cheese-ty'   and so on.

Fizz-buzz   Play as for Cheese. Forbidden numbers are now 3 and *multiples* of 3 (fizz) and 5 and multiples of 5 (buzz).

So 3 is fizz
     5 is buzz
     6 is fizz-fizz
     9 is fizz-fizz-fizz
    10 is buzz-buzz
    12 is fizz-fizz-fizz-fizz
    15 is buzz-buzz-buzz *or* fizz-fizz-fizz-fizz-fizz

Work with a partner   A and B.

(a) A experiments, making a variety of sounds. You will find that sound is amplified in the resonance cavities in the head. A feels and listens to the resonance of each sound. B aims to develop as resonant a tone as possible. Change over.

(b) A hums resonantly. B puts his head on A's back and feels the sound. Experiment with other sounds. Change over.

4 Silence is broken

Sit or lie in a circle. Eyes closed. Hold the silence. Teacher touches one person who shatters the silence with his own sound. Return to silence until someone else is touched.

More experienced students will be able to make sounds and hold silences at their own discretion.

Trust

Remembering names games

Introducing on my right ... Sit in a circle. If with a new group, go round the circle, each person introducing himself. Now start, 'Introducing on my right ...' and each person gives the name of whoever is on his immediate right. Then continue, 'Introducing on my right, but one ...' and each person says who is sitting next but one to him. Don't run on monotonously from 1 to 30, or whatever! Use this as a name reminder game whenever the group is sitting in a circle and you feel you need it, 'Introducing on my right, but ten ...'. 'Introducing on my right, but four ...', etc.

Signpost Sit in a circle. Have one person holding his arms out like a signpost in the middle. He or she closes eyes and spins until you call 'stop'. Signpost opens eyes and must say immediately which way his arms point – 'Mary – Richard'.

Throwing names Sit in a circle. One person starts, makes eye contact with another whose name he calls as he throws him an imaginary ball. That person catches the ball, makes eye contact with another whose name he calls as he throws the ball. And so on. No one may throw the ball to the same person twice! If someone is stumped for a name, he must make eye contact with the person and *roll* the ball to him. That person will hold the ball and say his own name, before rolling the ball back. The game then continues with the ball being thrown and the name called.

Essential exercises to make name-learning fun, introduce physical contact and liberate talk in a new group.

1 Initials

Work round the class. Each member introduces himself and then the other members of the class add something that he might like beginning with his initials, e.g.

John Brown

John Brown likes *J*am *B*utties ... *J*elly *B*abies ... *J*ust *B*eing ... *J*apanese *B*udgerigars ... *J*ourneying in *B*ulgaria ..., etc.

To add variety you can specify 'food', 'pleasant', 'unpleasant', 'absurd', 'to do with a country or place', etc.

2 Telegrams

(a) Send a telegram to one member of the class. Work round the class with each student contributing a word, e.g.

Pat Smith

*P*lease *A*rrange *T*ransport *S*aturday. *M*ust *I*nfiltrate *T*errorist *H*eadquarters.

(b) Divide quickly into groups of 5 or 6. Allow just one minute for each group to make up a telegram to send to a given person. Sound cymbal when one minute is up. Listen to telegrams. If they are not complete, ask the other groups to finish them.

3 Names and faces

Sit in a circle. One person starts, makes eye contact with someone else in the circle and chooses the perfect christian name for them. 'You look like an "Imogen" to me!' Other people in the circle offer suggestions and comments, 'No. Imogens have long hair! I think she's a "Sarah"', etc.
  This can be interesting if you really don't know the person's name!
  Try limiting the group to names of Shakespearian characters, characters from literature, mythology, etc.

Games to introduce physical contact in a new group

Mill and grab is an excellent mixing-up game and can be used to create random groups, or to liven up a lesson by breaking up existing groups and forming new ones.

Mill and grab   Call any number; say '5'. The class must immediately get into groups of 5. As a group forms, the members put their arms round each other to make a tight circle. Call another number, '8'. The class immediately re-forms into groups of 8. Call '30' (or however many you have in the class). Everyone makes contact in one large tight group!

Once the principle of the game is grasped, try variations, e.g.

move in slow motion, as if under water, so movement must be completed in one breath. Children 'drown' if they don't reach a group in time;

move with eyes shut, humming to indicate you are looking for a group. As groups form, humming stops;

move in silence, eyes open. Each group starts humming as soon as it is formed. As the members of the group run out of breath they are supported by the others until the group collapses slowly together.

Use adverbs to dictate the manner of moving – cheerfully, furtively, reluctantly, eagerly, etc.

Tangle   The whole group holds hands to link into a human chain. The first person slowly leads the chain through itself into a tight tangle. One person then untangles the group without breaking the chain.

Chase your tail   Work in groups of 6 or 8. Stand behind each other in a line with your hands on the waist of the person in front. Tuck a scarf in the belt of the last person. That is the dog's tail! The front person is the dog's head, and must run round in circles to catch his tail. When he succeeds, he moves to the end of the line and becomes the tail, and the front person starts chasing him. Encourage 'barking' as the chase is in progress!

4 | Surnames

Sit with a partner. A and B. A tells B his surname. B becomes the 'expert' and explains to him his definitive version of the derivation of the name. Or have a small group of 'experts' discussing the roots of one surname.

5 | Getting to know your partner

(a) **Earliest memories**   Work with a partner or in a small group and exchange your earliest memories. The group could act out one of these occasions. You might like to try a 'flashback' sequence in which, as one person recalls his or her story, another group simultaneously acts it out. Or the storyteller could start, setting the scene and characters, and then leave the flashback group to develop the story spontaneously.

(b) **Useful information!**   Sit with a partner. A and B.
A must find out four or five useful facts about his or her partner. Change over. Recap to fix the information. A must now find out four or five more facts. (These can be trivial details – colour of front door/brand of toothpaste used/etc.) Change over.
Now one partner may introduce the other to the rest of the class. Or leave this stage till the end of the lesson to see how much is remembered.

(c) **'In-depth' interviews**   Sit with a partner. A and B.
A asks questions in order to get to know his or her partner better – likes/dislikes/ambitions/etc. Change over.

(d) **Lie detector!**   Work in pairs or small groups. One tells the others a story about himself or herself. The other(s) decide whether it is true or not.

6 | Adopting roles

Sit facing a partner to form an outer and an inner circle grouping. B's in the outer circle question their partners (A's) in the inner circle for one or two minutes.
Outer circle moves round one place to face a new partner. A's now ask the questions but B's must answer in the character of the person they have just interviewed. If they don't know the answer to any question they must answer as they think their previous partner would have done. After a given time, B's move round the circle again. This time B's ask the questions and A's answer in the character of the person they last questioned.
At the end of the exercise, you can ask the final interviewer if he has any idea of the true. identity of his partner.

Squirrels in the trees Stand in groups of 3. A, B and C. A and B stand facing each other and hold hands to form the hollow trunk of a 'tree'. C is the 'squirrel', who gets into the 'tree' by ducking under A's and B's arms and standing between them! 'Trees' take up position. 'Squirrels' move about. At a sudden signal, which means 'danger!', they must rush into a hollow tree for safety! One squirrel per hole, and the same tree must not be used more than once by any squirrel!

Vampires Ideally, this game should be played in a darkened studio, but does work in daylight conditions if players have the self-discipline and nerve to keep their eyes shut. Everyone works 'blind' throughout the game. Just before the game starts, touch your 'vampires' (about 1 'vampire' to 5 'mortals'). 'Mortals' move slowly around the room trying to avoid physical contact. 'Vampires' move amongst them. When a vampire makes contact with a mortal, he holds his victim to him and whispers 'Blood!' in his ear. The victim screams and becomes a vampire! This new vampire now goes on his way in search of more human blood. If a vampire catches another vampire by mistake, the captive vampire does not scream but echoes the cry of 'Blood', and both vampires return to being mortal.

Human noughts and crosses Arrange nine chairs in a block or use squares on the floor as your noughts and crosses grid. Work in groups of 12 (5 noughts, 5 crosses, 2 players). Play exactly as for noughts and crosses, using human pieces. Noughts sit with hands on heads, crosses sit, arms crossed, in front of them.

7 **Make me laugh**

Work with a partner. A and B. A must try to make his partner laugh. When he succeeds, he gets up and moves to another A and tries to make him laugh. If you have a stolid, straight-faced A, B's can join forces to make him laugh. The exercise finishes when all the A's are laughing!

8 **What's best?**

Sit in a circle. Everyone looks at everyone else in the circle in turn, and *silently* considers what is the 'best thing' about each person – aspect of personality, a certain physical attribute, etc.

Developments

The rules of the tribe   Discuss how people show that they belong to a certain group, movement or gang – i.e. 'uniform', hairstyles, greetings, secret signs. What are the benefits of being part of a group? What are the dangers and disadvantages? Does everyone belong to a group?

In groups of 6 or 8 create a new 'society'. Choose a symbol, e.g. a style of greeting or a detail of dress, which everyone in the group adopts. Act out a short scene, e.g. meeting at someone's house or in a café. The others look for the group's special symbol. When one person thinks he knows what it is, he may try to join the group. Develop as spontaneous improvisation.

What's in a greeting   Observe the way people greet each other. What can we learn about them from their mode of greeting? Consider the variety of relationships within families, different cultures, social class, official manners, military etiquette, 'pecking' orders, different styles of salesmen and shopkeepers.

Develop this in improvisation, using a simple sequence of greeting to establish the *relationship* between the people concerned.

Use an opening greeting of 'Good morning' to establish the tone and mood of the rest of the sequence. (See Inflexion circles, p. 83.)

Examples: How do you say 'good morning' when you want to stop and talk, when you're in a hurry, when you can't tolerate the person you've met, or are frightened of him?

(See also What's in a smile?, p. 35.)

Symbols   Divide into groups of 5 or 6. Sit in a line behind each other. 'Brand' the person at the end of each line by gently making a symbol (letter/number/ square/circle/etc.) on his back. He passes on the symbol by writing it on the back of the person in front of him, who passes it on again until the whole line is 'branded'. Have a different symbol for each group. Quickly mix the groups with an energetic activity. 'Freeze and eyes shut.' Members of the original groups must find each other by writing their symbol in the hand of anyone they touch. If they 'match' they join hands and continue together, eyes shut. Each group sits when it thinks it is complete.

This game works well if the groups are 'branded' near the beginning of a lesson and asked to find each other just before the lesson finishes.

Code names   Work as for Symbols, but give each group a code word instead of a symbol. Later in the lesson, with eyes shut, groups must find each other by whispering the code to anyone they touch. Aim for the quietest whispers possible! Before opening eyes, groups should count their members to check that all members of the original secret gang are present.

Further ways of promoting physical contact and language using 'greetings' as a natural theme.

1 Greetings

Children need to remember the following sequence of greetings:

the 1st person you meet, you touch with one finger
    2nd person you meet, you touch with one finger from each hand
    3rd person you meet, you touch with one hand
    4th person you meet, you touch with both hands
    5th person you meet, you touch with your forearm
    6th person you meet, you touch with your shoulder
    7th person you meet, you touch with your forehead
    8th person you meet, you touch with your nose

then begin again, so the ninth person, you touch with one finger!

The class mixes and each member tries to greet as many people as possible. The fun and skill of this exercise comes when most people are at a different stage in the greeting sequence, so a child greeting his fourth person will offer his hands, but if that person has reached his seventh greeting the touch will be hands to forehead, not hands to hands.

2 Handshakes

Think of the ways people traditionally greet each other in different countries - the British handshake, the French kiss on both cheeks, the Indian 'How!', the Chinese bow, etc.

(a) In pairs (A and B) make up a *new* mode of greeting. Sit in two lines, A's facing B's. One A greets his or her partner, 'teaching' the greeting to the other A's so that they, in turn, can greet B's in the manner to which they are accustomed!

(b) Or play this as an observation game. A's must observe and copy *exactly*, otherwise their greeting will be rejected by B.

(c) Subtle 'secret' signs can be incorporated into the greetings.

(d) Work as for (a) in pairs. Each pair decides on a mode of greeting. Then one pair joins another pair. They teach each other their greeting and *combine* them. So if pair 1 clapped hands and pair 2 touched ears, the greeting now becomes, clap hands/touch ears. The four now meet up with another four and *combine* greetings again. Clap hands/touch ears/bend knees/turn around, or whatever! Can you continue until the whole class learns one composite greeting?

(e) Add sounds to the greeting to form a class chant. Think of the 'war chant' used by the All Blacks before a game.

'Who or what am I?' games with development into improvisation

Who or what am I?   One person decides Who or What he is, e.g. Nelson, the prime minister, a swimming pool, a spoon. He tells the others whether they must find out 'Who' or 'What'. They have one question each to discover his identity.

Celebrity guests   Write the names of 5 or 6 well known personalities on stick-on labels. Choose your celebrity guests and stick a name on each forehead. Let them mix with the rest of the class in party atmosphere. The others react to them according to the name on their forehead. How quickly can each 'personality' discover his or her own identity?

Set up the exercise as above but use 'collections' of objects, animals, towns, vegetables, etc. Invite the 'special guests' to a party. How quickly can they discover their identity and whether they're at the Vegetables' Ball, the Noah's Ark Reunion, or whatever?

Into groups   Prepare groups of names – sportsmen, historical figures, characters from Shakespeare, entertainers, mythological figures, etc. Give one to each member of the class and ask him to stick it on someone else's forehead without revealing the mystery identity. Let the group mix and chat and try to group into 'categories'. Obviously clues are gleaned by other people's reactions to you, not by asking direct questions about your identity.

When the class has organised itself into groups, ask each group to justify its membership. Are they all murderers? royalty? entertainers? contemporaries of each other? etc.

Use as a means of grouping for improvisation – perhaps to tell a story about a member of each group. Or presume that each group has landed in a time machine. What do they make of the current scene?

You might like to develop this sequence by separating into 'the living' and 'the dead'. Ask the dead where they think they are: Heaven or Hell? And ask the living where they think they'll go to! Presumably, there'll be some differences of opinion here – so hold a 'debate' and allow 'St Peter' to decide.

Choose about four people who are definitely on their way to Heaven or Hell (2 going to Heaven, 2 going to Hell is convenient!). The rest of the class now splits up to become welcoming parties at St Peter's gate or at the gates of Hell! They must think of a fitting treat or punishment for each of the new arrivals.

3   Parties

(a) **Finding out names**   Close eyes. Imagine you have something to eat in your left hand and something to drink in your right hand. Open eyes. You are all at a party. You have 30 seconds to find out as many names as possible and what everyone else is eating and drinking.

(b) **Liars' parties**

(i) Everyone assumes a character, the more outrageous the better, and boasts about his exploits.

(ii) *Crooks' party*   Everyone at the party is an 'ex-con'! Swop stories and tips.

(iii) *Huntin', shootin', fishin' party*   A chance to send up the upper class!

(iv) *Football supporters' club party*   Make admission exclusive – ticket only!

(v) *Weight-watchers' party*   Everyone has a weight problem!

(vi) *Allergics Anonymous*   Before the party everyone should acquire an allergy or phobia – to woollen clothing, to cheese, to people with red hair, to being touched, etc. See what happens when you get to the party! Discuss to discover if everyone's allergy was noted.

(vii) *International convention*   Choose a nationality and adopt the accent to go with it. Mix at the party and look for more of your compatriots. Or try the 'Save British Dialects' AGM.
(See Accents game, p. 86.)

(c) **Mixed parties**   Use four contrasting groups of people, say, crooks, 'toffs', allergy sufferers, and mixed nationals. Each group chooses a suitable venue for a party and starts to work in a corner of the room. Let the parties run until the characters within each group are established, and then move one or two people from each group on to the next one. These are *not* gate-crashers, and must be received civilly. Allow time for reaction to these newcomers, then send one or two more from each original group into the next group but one. And so on, until each group is completely mixed.

(d) **Introductions**   Start in pairs. A and B. A takes B to a party and, without discussing the matter, introduces him, e.g. 'Have you met John who's just come back from collecting spiders in the Amazon jungle?' B immediately accepts the description and reacts accordingly. As the conversation continues, A feeds in more information to complement B's reactions. Work in small groups so that the characters have a chance to develop. Change over.

Recognition by touch games

Play 'Who am I?' first, because here B has the control of placing A's hands. 'Who is it?' lacks this constraint and demands greater trust and sensitivity.

Who am I?   Divide the class into pairs. A and B. A's sit in a line on one side of the room, eyes shut. B's mix and choose an A to kneel in front of. B takes A's hand and allows him or her to touch clothing, face, hair – any 'clue' that he or she particularly wishes A to remember. B returns to the other side of the room and sits. A opens eyes and must move across the room to identify the person he was touching.

Who is it?   Form a circle. One person stands in the centre of the circle with eyes closed. He calls 'revolve' and the others move round him until he says 'stop'. People in the circle offer their hands to him. He moves 'blind', takes someone's hand and tries to guess who it is. If he cannot guess, he may feel clothing, face and hair and, finally, ask *one* question. 'Victim' may reply in disguised voice.

Find your partner   Work in pairs early in the lesson. Then do an energetic mixing activity. When class is mixed, call 'Freeze and eyes shut.' Original pairs must find each other *silently* by touch. Open eyes, move to side of room and sit when reunited.

Games practising sensitive movement and physical contact

Trains   Begin by working this game in twos or threes and, as confidence develops, combine groups to increase the length of the train.

Stand behind each other in a line, hands on the elbows of the one in front. All close eyes except for the train driver at the *back* of the train. Begin to shunt off very slowly. The driver directs by pressure on the elbows of the 'coach' in front. Pressure on right elbow means bear to the right, and the instruction is passed on down the line of coaches.

Have any number of trains working at once.

Suggest a rail track system with sidings, points and signals and appoint three or four guards and signal men to control all the train drivers.

Change drivers frequently, so that the experience of leading and being led is shared.

Exercises and games to introduce an awareness of pressure and encourage sensitive touch and trust between partners – essential *first steps* towards breaking the 'touch barrier'.

1 Feel

Working individually, and moving as little as possible, let your tongue feel your teeth, your feet feel your shoes, your wrists feel your cuffs, your neck feel your collar, your waist feel your belt, your finger feel the ring that's on it, etc.

2 Varying pressure of touch

(a) Find a space and sit down. Clench your fists and *squeeze* as hard as you can. Take a deep breath and say 'squ-e-e-ze' as you let your breath out. Now *stretch* your fingers and say 'str-e-t-ch'. Shake your fingers and relax.

(b) Close your fists as *lightly* and *slowly* as possible so you can hardly feel your fingertips on your palms. *Slowly* unfold your fingers.

(c) Let the fingertips of your right hand touch those of your left as *lightly* as possible. Try to hold the contact without varying pressure. Are certain fingers more sensitive or easier to control than others? Now try again, this time with your eyes shut.

(d) Sit facing a partner. A and B. Hold your hands up to each other so that your fingertips are as close as possible without touching. Now let all fingertips touch and hold the contact as lightly as you can.

(e) Sit facing a partner as for (d). Close eyes. A allows one finger of his or her right hand to make contact with the corresponding finger on B's left hand. B must copy the movement with his or her right hand. Hold the contact lightly. Now the initiative passes to B who may *break* contact or *make* contact with another finger of his or her right hand. A copies with his or her right hand, and so on.

3 Writing in hands

(a) Sit with a partner. A and B. A closes eyes and offers hand to B. B gently writes a letter in the palm of A's hand. A says what it is, eyes still closed. If it is the right answer, B continues, letter by letter, to write a word. Change over.

Traffic wardens   You need about 1 'warden' per 5 'cars'. Stand in a space. Eyes shut. Touch your traffic wardens, who open eyes. The 'cars' begin to move very slowly as if in a thick fog – no sound – arms folded in front. The traffic wardens must prevent *all* collisions, either car with car or car with furniture or wall, by taking the 'car' by the shoulders and guiding in a safe direction. If two cars collide, traffic wardens separate and redirect them. Play for 1 minute. Count the number of collisions. Change your traffic wardens. The most successful wardens are the ones with the least number of accidents!

The fence   Work in teams, about 6 or 8 to a team. Set up a row of chairs on their sides across the middle of the room – the fence! Each team chooses a pair of leaders. The others work with eyes shut. The leaders must take their team up to the fence and guide each member over it to safe territory the other side of the room. Anyone touching the fence is electrocuted and must remain where he dies. The team that crosses the fence with most survivors in the shortest time is the winner!

Use as a starter for an improvised escape story.

Touch and die!   The object of this game is to *avoid* touching! Start using the whole area of the room. Children weave in and out of each other avoiding contact. If two touch they 'die' together and freeze for the rest of the game.

Reduce the area allowed for movement. Have a signal which means 'reverse direction'. Call instructions, 'hop now', 'crawl', 'riding a bicycle', 'as puppets', 'witches', etc. Try working to music.

Contact with a 'dead' person can 'kill' so, as the bodies mount, and the area is reduced, and the movement pattern changed, the game becomes increasingly difficult.

When the class has got into the habit of weaving in and out skilfully, develop the exercise by giving an imaginative setting, e.g. clothes in a washing machine, currants in a fruit cake mix, snowflakes in a blizzard. Move as close as you can to each other without bumping. De-climax by slowing down gradually to 'stop'.

Or work Touch and die! in a small area, crawling on hands and knees and accepting that people will touch. When a conglomeration of bodies is formed, let the remaining members of the group stand back and look at it. What could it be? – a pile of rubbish – jetsam on the beach – a piece of sculpture – the remains of a house after a fire – bodies on a battlefield?

Develop in spontaneous improvisation, with either the onlookers or the 'mound' taking the initiative. If necessary, 'What a pity!' is a good opening line to give an onlooker.

(See also Building descriptions and stories, p. 149; Take a line p. 150.)

If partners do not know each other, use this exercise to write Christian names.

(b) Work in the same way to make a sentence, writing *alternate* words, e.g. A writes 'WE', B continues 'HAVE', A adds 'GOT', 'HISTORY', 'NEXT'. As confidence builds, encourage development from the mundane to the absurd.

(c) Write alternate letters to make a word.

(d) Write on each others' backs, legs and, finally, foreheads.

In this exercise, the game of 'writing messages' provides acceptable motivation for touching, and transition from the simple contact, hand on hand, to the more intimate, hand on face, is achieved easily with the natural development from writing on hands to writing on faces.

4 Leading the blind

(a) Work in pairs. A and B. B closes eyes. A takes B by the arm and slowly leads him or her around, as if helping a blind friend to get to know the geography of the room. A should *talk* quietly to B, drawing attention to potential difficulties and interesting features. Change over.

(b) Work in pairs, as above, but this time A does *not* talk to his blind partner as they move around the room. A should choose several features in the room for B to touch and explore. B must remember where A has taken him. Change over.

Discuss the reassuring quality of speech in this situation.

(c) Set a simple obstacle course – rostra to be climbed over, tables to be crawled under, chairs to avoid, etc. Work in pairs. A and B. B closes eyes. A leads his blind partner through the obstacles, all the time *talking* him through the journey.

(See also Exploring textures – Pair work (c), p. 117.)

5 Leading with one finger

(a) Work in pairs. A and B. Make light contact, forefinger to forefinger. B closes eyes. A leads his partner around the room, controlling and guiding solely by the pressure of his fingertip. The finger-to-finger link must not be broken. Change over.

(b) Work as above, but this time A's *exchange* partners. Keep the movement slow and the changes positive. Make several changes in one sequence. Before B's open eyes, can they say who their new partners are?

Let them feel hands – arms – shoulders – face – and, if necessary, listen to voice before saying who it is.

Developments in improvisation

'Make-up' leading to character work   Sit with a partner. A and B. A is going to 'make-up' B's face with imaginary make-up – clown, Red Indian, puppet, monster, etc. A must *explain* to B what colours he is using, what effects he is trying to achieve as he works. B repeats activity, talking to A and making-up A's face so they are *identical*. Identical partners move together, mirroring each other's speech and actions. (See Basic mirror work, p. 17; Mirror speech, p. 23.)

Repeat, but now create different *character* make-ups so you have pairs of contrasting or complementary characters. Characters question each other in pairs to find out as much as possible about each other. To deepen characterisation, *you* may ask detailed questions – age? occupation? clothes? likes? dislikes? Everyone answers at once, talking quietly into hands. (See Talking into hands, p. 77.)

Link into 4's or 6's. Give a time and a place (e.g. dawn at Stonehenge; 5.00 p.m. at the Bus Station), and allow characters to improvise spontaneously. A progressive improvisation technique may be useful here. (One person starts, others join in one by one.) However absurd or fantastic the situation may seem to be, ensure that the characterisation is sustained with sincerity.

Finally, sitting with a new partner from that group, remove each other's make-up, talking as you do so.

Older students may create very *subtle* character make-ups and adapt them as the characterisations develop. Art work and practical use of stage make-up arise naturally after this exercise.

Character from texture   Everyone should choose a texture in the room to explore with eyes closed. Consider the texture in terms of *personality*. Think how often we use adjectives describing texture to describe character – smooth, abrasive, fluffy, etc. Use question/answer technique (as above) to extend the characterisation. Set up a large group situation such as a party, and require characters to mix and talk about themselves. Encourage grouping of like characters. Finally, out of character, discuss the collection of *textures* found in each group.

Touch exercises exploring texture and encouraging students to make imaginative associations relating to touch and texture.

1 Exploring textures - individual work

(a) Feel the different textures of your clothing.

(b) Feel the different textures on your hands and on your face.

(c) Look for *similar* textures. Consider *degrees* of roughness and smoothness. What is the smoothest surface in the room?

Talk about your findings.

2 Exploring textures - pair work

(a) Sit with a partner. A and B. A closes eyes and offers forefinger to B. B gently takes finger and places it somewhere on his own *clothing*. A must guess what part of B's clothing he is touching. Keep pressure light and allow very little movement of fingertip. Change over and repeat several times.

(b) Working with the same partner, A closes eyes and offers finger to B. B places finger on his own *face*. A must guess what part of B's face he is touching. Change over and repeat.

Encourage pairs to talk *quietly* after each attempt.

(c) Stand up. A closes eyes. B leads A around the room *slowly* and *carefully*. B takes A's finger and places it on any *surface* in the room. A guesses what he is touching. Change over and repeat several times using different parts of the body to explore the textures in the room, e.g. touching with wrists only, elbows only, bare feet, noses. Discuss in pairs.

3 Exploring textures - group work

(a) Sit in small circles of 4 or 5. Close eyes. Place an object in the middle of each circle. Object is passed around group, each person commenting on its texture, shape, use, etc., until they reach *agreement* on what it is or what it *might* be.

(b) Place a piece of costume or material in each circle. Students feel and describe it until they reach agreement and, finally, eyes still closed, decide what *colour* they think it is.

Journeys   Use a follow-the-leader technique with an inexperienced group. Work in groups of 5 or 6 and number 1–6 before starting. The first student starts the journey, say, through a wood: 'Mind the branches'. The others follow, joining in: 'Watch those brambles', etc. Then number 2 becomes the leader: 'It's becoming very swampy', and so they all journey on into the swamp. When he or she feels the time is right, number 3 takes over: 'We've got to get across that river'; and so on, until everyone in the group has taken the lead.

Encourage *fantastic* journeys where surfaces can change and one can fly, swim under the ocean, float in space – in fact, where *anything* can happen!

With a little experience the group will share the lead freely, no longer needing to work in a set order. (See Building descriptions and stories, p. 149.)

Game

Blind detectives   Have a number of objects in readiness – household objects, headgear, toys, stage properties. A diverse collection works best. Work in pairs. A and B. B closes eyes. Very quickly arrange the objects around the room. A's then lead their blind partners to feel and identify the objects. Two or three can work on the same object. B's may talk, but A's should not give any hints. At a given signal, the A's lead their blind partners to sit together in a group. A's quickly remove the assorted objects and sit down. Eyes open. B's consult and agree on a list of the objects they touched. A's may ask questions, e.g. 'Was it an *electric* kettle?' 'What do you think the crown was made of?', 'Did the bicycle have gears?' or, if the B's are uncertain about an object, 'What do you think it was *for*?' Change over using different objects. This is an exercise that can well be set up by half the class for the others.

A detective story could evolve using the 'clues'. Work in groups and plan a story incorporating all the objects found in the room.

4 | Awareness of texture

Pair work   Collect interesting textures – small pieces of fur, materials, feathers, teazles, conkers, polythene, rubber. (Ask the children to bring them in.) Each child finds something with which to test his partner. Sit in pairs (A and B). A shuts eyes. B touches him with whatever he has chosen. A must guess what it is.

Group work   Collect containers of 'textures' – cornflakes, holly leaves, rice, paper clips, water. Place all containers under a length of curtaining. Children come in groups to *feel* but must not look. They sit back in their groups and discuss what they think is there. When they have agreed, they *memorise* their list. Listen to all the lists. Then uncover the containers and check.

   Half the class can prepare a similar 'test' for the other half. Most of the fun, and the discovery, is in the preparation!

5 | Recall

(a) *Touch* and handle warm dry sand, cold wet sand, a kitten, a snake, a slug, flour, plasticine. Plunge your hand into cold porridge, treacle, a bag of feathers. Turn on the hot tap and then the cold tap, feel the water.

(b) *Add sound*, e.g. a yawn when handling the sand, a squelching noise when drawing hand out of porridge.

(c) *Eat* candy floss, sticky toffee, fat ham, crisp crackling savouring the texture of the food. Peel an orange and spit the pips, nibble at hard-to-crack brazil nuts, peel a banana. Taste and smell the food as you eat it!

(d) *Walk* on different surfaces – shingle, slime, a ledge hundreds of metres above the sea, a trampoline, a magnetic floor. Create a 'nightmare room' where the floor constantly changes texture, and the inhabitants change size.

(e) **Work with a partner**   A and B. A is stranded in mud, quicksand, a vat of toffee, a deep well, a room where patches of the floor are red hot, where the floor is covered with itching powder, in the middle of a frozen lake, in a giant spider's web, halfway up the rainbow. B must rescue him.

   Repeat in slow motion, or use slow motion as a control at any time during the exercises.

Developments

Change-over snapshots   Divide the class into pairs of matching groups, i.e. a group of 5 is matched by another group of 5, one of 6 is matched by another of 6. Each group forms a 'snapshot' taken on holiday. Matching groups sit facing each other. A and B. The first person in Group A takes his corresponding number in Group B and moulds him into the position that he held in the Group A photograph. A2 moulds B2, and so on, until Group B forms A's photograph. Let the photograph come to life. Is the action and characterisation as A intended? Do the people in the photograph know who they are and what their relationship is? Discuss. Then change over so that Group B moulds Group A.

Comic strip   Select a few frames from a comic strip cartoon and use as the framework for a scene. Specify that these are the beginning, middle and final frames.

Work in small groups. Look at the frames you have been given. Decide the order they should go in, and make up your own links to complete the story. In presentation, start frozen in the positions of your first frame, improvise the link to the next frame and freeze again, improvise to the final scene and finish *still*.

This tight structure is particularly useful with a difficult or insecure group.

When the idea of moving from one set point to another is accepted, groups can create their own cartoon strips of 4 or 5 frames (drawn as stick men or moulded in frozen movement) which can be brought to life with linking movement and dialogue.

Try an educational film strip illustrating an aspect of a sport or hobby.

Sculpting exercises to develop trust and acceptance of another person's ideas, literally, by putting yourself in someone else's hands.

1 Sculpting

(a) Work with a partner. A and B. Give a subject for a statue – famous person, nursery rhyme character, emotion. A is pliable clay and B is able to mould him into the shape of the statue. At a given signal A's come to life. Change over.

(b) Use a warm-up activity to start. Call freeze. All class relax except for the 'model' who is to be copied. Model must remain frozen, as if stone, throughout. Work in pairs, A sculpting B. Concentrate on detail – the angles of the fingers, expression, etc. At a signal, sculptors sit down. Model comes to life and walks around the exhibition of his doubles.

(c) Throw a piece of rope onto the floor in the centre of the room. Work in 4's – 1 sculptor, 3 'clay'. Sculptor moulds his clay into the shape of the rope. Change sculptors at each throw.

(d) Work in a large circle. Give a title – The Heroes, Hellfire, Sloth, Simplicity. The first person moves into the circle and positions himself as he thinks fit. He is pliable clay. The second person is a sculptor who may mould the clay into a more satisfying shape. The third person is another sculptor who observes and adjusts the shape already made – maybe looking at it from a different angle. The fourth person is clay and positions himself touching the existing shape. The fifth and sixth people are sculptors. And so on round the circle in sequence – clay, sculptor, sculptor – until everyone is part of the composition.
    It is important to work quickly in this exercise, or the first people begin to feel the strain! Allow only one or two adjustments per sculptor.
    Let the sculpture 'explode' in slow motion, and then reform, again in slow motion. It may be helpful to number the elements of the composition and call them out slowly, in reverse order, before regrouping them.

(e) Half the class is clay. The other half are sculptors working corporately on a large 3-D design to be viewed in the round. Encourage discussion as the sculptors decide how to tackle the problem. Watch the natural leaders emerge! Change over.

2 Frozen movement

(a) Work in groups of four or five. One sculptor, four models or 'stickmen'. The idea is to produce a series of 'stills' of one action, perhaps an athlete on his marks and beginning to run. The four models put

Monster Work in large groups, subdivided into sculptors and clay. The sculptors mould their clay into a monster. They breathe life into it. It moves. They give it sound. It makes noises. They tame it with signals. It becomes a friend. They learn how to communicate with it.

Develop in improvisation.

(See also Controlling with sound and Controlling with code, p. 63.)

themselves roughly in position one behind the other, and the sculptor adjusts the angles of head and body to achieve a smooth movement sequence. He will need to do the complete movement himself to get the feel of it. Don't neglect faces. Other actions to try are putting a coat on, getting into the bath, opening and using an umbrella in a gale, drinking a can of coke, tennis service, the catch – fishing or cricket!

Change over so that everyone has the chance to be the sculptor.

(b) Double up the groups and work in *pairs* on rugby tackle, at the hairdresser's, disco dance, the fight, tango. Remember there is no movement! Just a series of sculpted, frozen actions.

Games

Pair statues   A version of musical statues played in *pairs*. Move around with a partner until the music stops or a signal is given to freeze. *Immediately* and *without discussing it,* make a statue to represent whatever is called. Call the title of the statue and then count '4-3-2-1: Freeze!' Prepare lists of 'pairs' – Romeo and Juliet, Tom and Jerry, Knife and Fork, Bacon and Egg, Bread and Butter, Day and Night, Right and Left, Upstairs and Downstairs, Song and Dance, Summer and Winter, etc.

Numbers or letters, 'shapes' such as diamond, circle, star, and 'points and patches' can be used in a statue game once the students have experienced making the shapes. (See Making shapes, p. 133.)

In the *game* of statues, the emphasis is on quick reaction, co-operation and acceptance.

Stuck in the mud!   Have one 'catcher' per ten 'runners'. If the catcher touches a runner, the runner must freeze, feet apart, 'stuck in the mud'. He is freed if another runner can crawl through his legs. If the rescuer is caught 'in the act', he freezes immediately in front of his friend, hoping that someone will be able to rescue them both in one go! The catchers win if everyone is 'stuck in the mud'.

Develop personal discipline and control by 'playing' in slow motion. In slow motion games there is mutual acceptance between catcher and caught. The emphasis is on the pleasure of playing and *sharing* the game, not the winning or losing.

Statue work – introducing essential control factors and use of levels, and expanding to advanced sequences promoting quick, lateral thinking.

You'll find Melting, Blowing up and Growing and Sinking to numbers very useful exercises, providing a secure and *controlled* starting or finishing sequence to all statue work.

1 Freeze!

Before you tackle any statue work, children *must* be used to obeying the command 'Freeze!' *instantly*, and maintaining stillness until told to relax.

Make a *game* out of it.

He who moves after the music stops is out! (See Moving to music games, p. 44.)

Freeze at the signal and see how long you can *stay* still. Play this with a partner. See who moves first.

Try to achieve a 'frozen' classroom. Everyone must be still for a set time, say, 15 seconds, to start with. Use a stop watch. No one must move a muscle!

2 Melting

(a) Working individually, imagine you are a jelly on a hot-plate and are slowly melting from the bottom.

(b) Imaging you are an ice cream left out in the sun and you're melting from the top.

(c) Work in pairs. A and B. A forms B into a wax statue, and then melts him with a heat gun! B melts wherever the heat is directed. Change over.

3 Blowing up

Imagine you are a balloon lying on the floor. You are going to be 'blown up' to the count of 10. Float. Now release the pressure so the air rushes out.

Use this 'blowing up' technique to reform statues that have 'melted'.

Developments

Photographs   Make a collection of interesting pictures of pairs or small groups of people. Distribute them to the class. A picture with four people in it goes to a group of four. Groups form a 'still' of the picture and then, at a given signal, bring it to life. Encourage children to look for detail in the picture and subtle clues to character and situation.

At Christmas time, use old cards and let each group make a speaking Christmas card for the rest of the class.

Use a photograph to form the *final* tableau of a short scene.

Photographs are useful with children who find it difficult to get started in group work, however thorough your pre-experience work might have been! With a photograph there is something to latch onto straight away – an obvious and safe starting point.

(See also Comic strip, p. 120.)

Group statues   Sit in a circle. 'Build' a composite, three-dimensional statue on a given subject, e.g. cave, oak tree, tunnel, arch. Let the first person take up his position, then the second, and so on. *Don't discuss what you are doing.* Let the shapes you are making speak for themselves. Rebuild the statue to share it with the rest of the class and involve other groups, e.g. add people exploring the cave, sheltering under the tree, etc.

Try an *underwater* scene with a shipwreck, strange rocks and seaweeds, giant clams (that may trap divers!). Half the class forms the underwater scene. The rest are divers. Develop in improvisation.

Use abstract or unusual *titles* for your group statues. Try Heat wave, Strange god, Spaghetti junction, Suspension bridge, Hanging gardens, Mythological beast.

Create *exhibits* for a gallery of modern art. Invite the class to give a name to the exhibit. Invite the artist (anyone from the class) to talk about his work, or find an art critic to discuss it. Eavesdrop on two American tourists visiting the gallery.

4 | Growing and sinking to numbers

(a) 'Grow' into a statue to the count of five in five jerky movements. Specify the statue – tennis champion, skater, astronaut, double-bass player. Now bring the statue to life, in slow motion.

(b) Grow into a statue to the count of ten or fifteen, so slowly and smoothly that one is hardly aware of movement.

(c) Sink, using either of the above techniques. (b) Is particularly effective and demands considerable control and concentration.

(d) Work (a) and (b), this time, in *pairs*. Do not allow discussion. A must take his cue from the direction B begins to move in, and vice-versa. Try moving by numbers to make a pair statue of 'Shoe shop', 'Rescue', 'In the Wild West', 'At the dentist's'.

5 | Levels

(a) **Tall/wide/small/long** Fir tree (tip-toe, arms raised to point above head), Oak tree (arms spread, solid base), Acorn (curled up, round), Ivy (standing on one leg with other leg and arms stretched parallel to ground).

Use as a class warm up. Call 'Tall'. Everyone stretches. 'Small'. Everyone crouches, curled up, etc.

(b) **See-saw** Stand facing a partner. A and B. As A bends his knees, B stretches. As B returns to normal stance and begins to bend knees, A begins to stretch up. Practise until you are working together in perfect balance.

Try jumping so that A is on the ground as B is in the air!
(See Opposite mirrors and Grotesques, p. 19.)

(c) **Snake charmer** Work with a partner. A and B. A lies on his back. His arms and legs are the snakes. B is the snake charmer and controls the snakes by playing his pipe! Change over.

(d) **Squash** Work as a whole class. Imagine the ceiling is being lowered slowly to the count of ten, to squash you. Resist and be pushed down by the weight of the ceiling.

Now work with a partner. Imagine you are both trying to get a large feather mattress into a small box.

Work with a partner again. *Without touching*, use a 'force' from your hands to crumple your partner until he is cowering on the ground, completely overshadowed by you. Change over.

Nursery rhymes Work in groups. Give each group a nursery rhyme. They must tell the story in four pictures. Discipline the groups to change from one picture to the next without talking. Use a cymbal roll or tambour beat during the changes. Can the other groups guess what the nursery rhyme is?

Class statue scenes Give a title, 'The Rose and Crown on Saturday night', 'Back-stage', 'The deathbed', 'The big top', 'Crown Court'. *Everyone* freezes in position as a character in the scene. At a signal bring the scene to life. Background music – honky-tonk, orchestra tuning up, bell tolling, circus music, etc., will help to set the atmosphere. Encourage *interaction* between the characters, and develop as spontaneous improvisation. With a large group, you're likely to get several areas of action so, afterwards, discuss the different characters' involvement in the scene so that everyone can appreciate the improvisation as a whole.

Servant/master Use *levels* as the key to who is dominant and who is submissive. Work in pairs, A and B. Decide on character, relationship and situation. Agree who is to be dominant first. If A starts, he might stand while B is sitting, perhaps telling him off about something. If B can persuade A to sit and he can stand, B will become dominant. Make eye contact and freeze momentarily to emphasise the moment of change-over. Partners need to *cooperate* with each other, within reason, to share the servant/master roles. This works well with a few rostra blocks and step units ranged around the drama room.

(See Servant/master, p. 157.)

6 Group work on levels

(a) Stand in a space, eyes closed. Choose a 'level' – high (stretched tall), medium (knees bent) or low (crawling) and get into position. Eyes open. Move in slow motion towards someone else on your level, avoiding people at different levels, until the three groups are separated. Relax.

With younger children use 'giraffes', 'lions' and 'snakes' for high, medium and low.

(b) Repeat the exercise, adding *sound* to suit your level. Listen to the sounds of each group.

(c) Sit in small circles. The first person moves into the circle and takes up a high shape, the second takes up a medium shape touching the first person, the third makes a low shape touching the second person, the fourth makes a high shape touching the third person, and so on!

Avoid a proscenium arch approach. Remember you are working in the round and the final shape should be interesting from all sides.

(d) Work the exercise as above but, this time, everybody must make contact with everyone else!

(e) Add sound – a different note for each level.

(f) Let the statue break up with a slow motion 'explosion'. Then bring it together again by reversing the action, again in slow motion. Is everyone in exactly the same position?

Or let the statue 'melt' and then have life 'blown' into it again at the count of ten.

7 Justifying

A valuable exercise developing the ability to 'think on your feet!' and react immediately.

(a) Set the class working on some energetic activity – painting the floor and ceiling, working in the garden.

Call 'Freeze! … You are now an athlete in the Olympic games caught in action by our high-speed camera. Come to life, in slow motion, now!' Each child must use the frozen position he finds himself in as a starting point for the new movement activity.

(b) Allow the athletes to move in slow motion. Then call 'Freeze' again. This time the children choose for themselves how to 'justify' the position, e.g. an athlete caught, arm raised, after shot-put might decide he is now a policeman on point duty. The rule is – keep the same position but find another motivation for the movement.

Holiday slides   Work in groups of 4 or 5. One person in each group is showing the slides, the others are people in the photographs. The slide operator starts, 'This one is Auntie Mary feeding the ducks at Bognor.' Immediately the 'slide' takes up position as Auntie Mary and the ducks. Photographer can add any more comments he wishes to make about the slide. Slide remains frozen. Next slide. Now count 1–2–3–4–5, giving time for the photograph to *regroup*. At 5 the slide freezes, and the photographer must take his cue from the 'slide'. 'Ah yes, that's on the boat – Auntie Mary again and Grandad and young Jim in their life-jackets.' Next slide. Count again, for the picture to relax. At 5 the photographer gives the cue, 'This is a good one, at the zoo ...'. So the initiative passes from 'slide' to photographer alternately.

Don't allow the 'slide' to talk during the sequence, but afterwards let language flow as they discuss what the pictures were *meant* to be!

Changing channels   Work a similar sequence to Holiday slides, using the idea of changing channels on television. This is a little more difficult as the 'frozen group' will need to bring the scene to life with dialogue and movement! Again, initiative passes between viewer(s) and 'television set'.

Climax   Groups play out a short scene on a given theme. Others watch and listen. Discuss to discover the climax of the scene. Replay scene, appointing a director who makes any amendments necessary. At the climax, he 'freezes' the scene – 'takes a photo'. Observe faces, eye lines, grouping, and discuss.

(c) Work in pairs - putting in a window pane, moving the sideboard, folding a sheet, pushing a car that has stalled. Call 'Freeze, and justify!' Each pair must find a new meaning for their movement. Encourage speech as *part of the action*, but don't allow discussion.

8   Movement pun sequence

(a) Work sitting in a circle grouping. Two people (A and B) move into the centre of the circle. Specify what they are doing - washing the car, having a picnic, etc. People in the circle look for any action by A or B that is a 'movement pun'. As soon as someone spots an action that could be reinterpreted, he claps his hands and A and B freeze. He then moves into the centre of the circle and takes the place of A or B, whichever he is copying. The initiative is then with him. He must indicate how he wishes the scene to continue, e.g. if you had given 'shoe shop' as a starting idea, and A had sat down to try on shoes with B on his knees as the assistant, someone could take the place of A and continue the scene with 'Stay on your knees, serf. Beg for mercy ...'. As soon as someone else sees a 'movement pun', he can clap his hands. The action freezes and he moves into the circle. So the sequence could continue with someone replacing the prostrate serf and continuing, 'I've lost my contact lens, down this grating, here.'

(b) This is a progressive sequence to work with a group of 10–12. Start the seqence with one person doing any activity he chooses. As soon as someone sees a 'movement pun' he claps his hands to freeze the action, and moves in to develop the sequence. So, if the first person had been writing a letter and was just licking the envelope, the next person could come in, 'You'll be ill if you eat any more of that *melon.*' They continue the scene until someone else spots a movement pun. He then freezes them both, and comes in to dictate new action. And so on, until everyone in the group has joined in.

Developments

Spiders and starfish   Work in groups of 4, 5 or 6. Kneel down in a circle, heads together. Legs become tentacles or spiders' legs. Establish a movement pattern and add sound, e.g. raising the trunks in the air and adding a sucking sound as they are lowered to the ground, for a starfish.

Create creatures with personality – a sulky jellyfish, a mischievous spider, a star-struck starfish. Personality must be expressed mainly in backs and legs, and in sound.

Fantastic animals   In groups 'build' a fantastic animal. Think whether it has fur, feathers, scales or whatever you wish. What colour(s)? Habitat? Food? What sound does it make? One person in each group should be the 'keeper' and know all about his animal.

Sit in a circle. Each keeper presents his animal to the seated gathering who may ask questions and may be called upon to think of a name for the fantastic animal. Let spontaneous improvisation develop – someone may wish to buy or steal the animal for some purpose, the animal may possess magical properties, etc.

'Rebuild' all the animals. The keepers form one group to make an animal themselves. Each animal is from an unknown world, meeting other creatures for the first time. Music and lighting help to create a still, unearthly atmosphere which prohibits fighting. Use slow motion or 'weightlessness' as an extra control factor. Work into pairs. One of the animals in each pair is to 'eat' the other, as if in a dream, in slow motion. The animal that has been eaten serves to enlarge the other. Continue until there is one animal left in the room.

After this experience, talk about and recreate mythological beasts.

The message!   Suppose the whole class has crashed in the desert! How quickly can you arrange your bodies on the ground to make the message SOS or HELP! for an approaching aircraft to read?

You might divide the class into two groups, and see which half tackles the problem most efficiently!

Exercises to motivate uninhibited physical contact and imaginative use of the body.

During these exercises encourage discussion and decision-making in the group. Encourage groups to look for alternative ways of solving the same problem.

1 Numbers and letters

(a) **Hands and feet** Working individually, choose a number and draw it in the air – very large, very small. Trace it on the ground with your toe. Balance on one leg and write it in the air. Slowly, walk it on the floor, taking care not to bump into anyone.

(b) **Bodies** Working individually, use your whole body to become the shape of the number that is called. Work vertically or horizontally. Call 'easy' numbers first, like '1' and '7', then progress to '5' and '3'.

(c) **In pairs** Work together to make the shape of the number. Try '11', '8', '4', '12'.

(d) **In small groups** make numbers such as '102', '439', '888'.

(e) **In large groups** make a sum to suit a given number, e.g. '16' could be represented as '4 × 4' or '10 + 6'. Plus and minus signs, etc. should be made by bodies.

(f) Work a similar sequence with *letters*. Begin with initials and progress to spelling names.

2 Points and patches

(a) Working individually, balance on 'points' and 'patches' as instructed. Hands, feet, elbows, knees, heads are points. Backs, forearms, buttocks, etc. are patches. Call instructions, e.g. '1 point, 1 patch' or '4 points, 2 patches'. Class works accordingly.

(b) Working in pairs, repeat the exercise, sharing the ration of points and patches between people.

(c) Develop by gradually increasing the size of the group.

Ideas for using machines

What does it make?   Create a machine for a specific purpose. See if the rest of the class can work out what it does.

Trade Fair/Ideal Home Exhibition   Organise an exhibition where all the new inventions may be demonstrated to prospective purchasers.

Marketing sequence   Decide on a product. Divide class into two groups – 'manufacturing' and 'marketing'. The manufacturing group creates the machine that will make the product. The marketing group concerns itself with the advertising campaign and ideas for special promotions. Develop in improvisation.

Town hall clock   Design a big town hall clock. What happens on the hour?

'Emmit' designs   Design an 'Emmit' mousetrap, or an alarm-clock-cum-teamaker!

Tape recorder   Make a tape recorder. Link with Making a tape, p. 60.

Time machine   Make a time machine and use it!

Magic machine   Make a magic machine that turns people into frogs. How do you turn the frogs back into people?

Exercises in machine-making to develop physical cooperation and facilitate close involvement of the entire group.

1 Making machines

Altogether, make any noise that a machine might make. Try a different noise – and another.

Choose one of your noises and add a repeated mechanical action to fit it. Use your whole body, not just arms and legs! You'll find that the noise stimulates the action, and the action furthers the noise!

Find a partner. Demonstrate your noises and actions to each other and link them so you become adjacent parts of the same machine. Can you make the action of one prompt the movement of the other?

Now work with another pair and combine to form a larger machine.

Move on into groups of eight. You can amend the individual actions and sounds, if necessary, to give variety. Think about levels and contrasting sounds. Try to find a natural rhythm for your machine.

Practise until your machine is working smoothly!

Now present the machines one at a time, using the following exercises to increase concentration and audience participation.

(a) Watch one machine for a while. Then take out *one* person, saying that this section has broken down and must be replaced by an identical part. Another member of the class steps in, and the machine continues.

(b) Number parts of each machine, 1–8. Like numbers 'understudy' each other. Set up one machine. A part 'breaks down', but this time only the *sound* is missing. The corresponding numbers in the class supply the correct sound, and the machine continues.

(c) Develop these exercises so that no parts of the original machine remain, or so that the machine is working silently, its noises made by the rest of the class.

2 Factory noises

Find a space and sit down. What noise would you expect to hear coming from a factory that makes ping pong balls? (the composite class sound is the right noise!)

Add individual actions to suit the sound. An experienced group may react spontaneously with one another.

Try factories that make treacle toffee, steel girders, crystal chandeliers, ice cream, micro-chips, fly spray.

Progress to factories that make false teeth for giants, or spectacles for mice! What does a 'think-tank' sound like? Or a 'dream-machine'?

Abstract machines   Create an *'emotion machine'*, or a *'seasons machine'*, or a *'weather machine'*.

The machine parts use symbolic gesture and phrases, rather than the essentially mechanical movement and sound of the previous machines, e.g. a *'hate machine'* would presumably have parts that stamped feet or shook fists and would shout and hiss;

a *'rain machine'* might have a part that repeatedly put up an umbrella and said 'Rain again'. Another part might set up a time beat with an onomatopoeic 'drip-drop, drip-drop'.

Try a *'dream machine'* that reacts according to information fed into it.

3   **Quick machines**

When the group is reasonable experienced at machine-making, set them working *quickly* in fours to make the following machines with moving parts. Give a strict time limit. (Count down from 10 to 1). Or, ask for *no* talking, so that agreement must be reached with maximum use of eye contact and non-verbal communication.

Use food mixer, record player, tape recorder, bicycle, cuckoo clock, helicopter, typewriter, or sewing machine as ideas.

Developments

Create *stories concerning puppets*, such as this one.

All the puppets are in the puppet-maker's workshop – one puppet is almost human – witch wants it – puppet-master will not sell – witch steals puppet – puppet-master finds that wood shavings from 'human' puppet have magical properties – sprinkled over other puppets they free speech and movement – puppet-master and puppets go together on journey in search of stolen puppet.

Try to use the characteristics of all the puppets on the journey –

the clockwork mouse can get through narrow places
the puppet on a spring can see over walls
the bear can climb trees
the strong-man can lift great weights
the clown can make people laugh
the dancer can charm
the fairy can fly, etc.

They find the witch's hide-away. How do they retrieve their friend? If they use force the witch might turn them all into deathwatch beetles! (If this happens, presumably someone somewhere has an antidote!) Anyway, why did the witch want the puppet in the first place – as a slave, or as a companion? Could the witch be of any assistance to the puppet-maker?

The end of the story is up to the class!

Robots' restaurant   Imagine a restaurant or fast food shop run by robots!

Divide class into two. Half are humans eating out in the restaurant. The others are robots and should sub-divide into cooks and waiters.

Discuss for a few minutes. What is on the menu? How do the robots communicate with each other and with humans? What are the robots' limitations? Why do the humans come to this restaurant? – It's very popular! Is there a human behind the robots?

Set up the kitchen and dining tables and run the scene.

Imaginative exercises to promote confidence in working together within a fairly tight, simple structure. Developments, however, can be advanced, demanding sophisticated assessment of behaviour.

1 Puppets

Working individually, think of a painted, wooden puppet face – a witch, a doll, a soldier, Mr Punch, etc.

Let that puppet's face take over your face. Move about as that puppet. Take that face off, and replace it with a different puppet face. Move again.

Suppose you are all *string* puppets. How do string puppets move? Where are the strings attached? Collapse onto the floor. Using a sharp beat as a signal for movement, pull the puppets up to the count of ten. Move in time with the beats.

Or have one sound to pull up a string, another to drop. You can specify the string that is being pulled or dropped – left wrist string, right knee string, head string – or just use the sound signal.

Find a partner. One is puppet, the other puppet-master. Puppet-master stands on a chair, puppet is collapsed on the floor. Master lifts puppet by imaginary strings. Work closely, so that puppet can anticipate his master's action, and master allows for the natural flow of movement of his puppet.

2 Clockwork

Think of a clockwork toy. Wind up the mechanism to the count of five. Now move. Use the rattle of castanets as a control. Start fast and gradually slow to stillness.

Work in pairs to make a clockwork toy with two moving parts, e.g. a girl giving a bone to a dog who begs for it, two soldiers saluting, two clowns, etc. Practise your sequence. Remember that every movement must look mechanical and that you must return to your set start-position in order to repeat your sequence.

Watch the toys, using another member of the class to wind each one up, and controlling the 'running down' of the clockwork with castanets, as above.

People into puppets   Instead of thinking of puppets becoming more human, consider the reverse – people turning into puppets! On most days the News will offer copious examples.

Who are the puppet-masters? How firmly are the strings attached? What are the advantages/disadvantages of being a puppet? Maybe we are all puppets controlled by 'Fate'?

Develop in discussion and improvisation.

Punch and Judy   Take a typical Punch and Judy scenario, e.g. Mr Punch uses his 'slap-stick' to kill the dog (who steals the sausages), the baby (who cries), Mrs Punch (who shouts at him), the beggar (who wants food), the doctor (who prescribes unsavoury medicine), the policeman (who is asking questions), the magistrate (who convicts him), the hangman (who is tricked into putting his head in his own noose). Finally, when the devil is after him, Punch just manages to escape to fight another day!

Set this up as a children's beach show (using life-size puppets), with the audience laughing at the 'incredible' characters and storyline. The audience returns home in family groups.

Watch them at home. Was the Punch and Judy show so incredible? Look for parallel behaviour patterns in relationships, prejudices, reactions. Work out in improvisation.

Life-size pieces   Play a game with human counters, chess pieces, cards, etc.

(See Human noughts and crosses, p. 106.)

If playing a board game, it is probably easier for the players not to handle their life-size pieces. Set the players (working with imaginary counters) in one area, and enlarge the action using the life-size counterparts. This demands maximum awareness between groups, e.g. if a player picks up a piece, the life-size counterpart must react.

Naturally, the counters or cards can speak and discuss their masters' strategies, manners, fingernails! This is not heard by the players who continue their game. There may come a moment when the pieces control the players, in a grand role-reversal.

Parallels   Look for 'real-life parallels' to children's games. Start by playing the game as children and let the action move out of the safe confines of the game into observations of adult life. Try 'I'm the king of the castle', 'Follow the leader', 'The farmer's in his den', 'Snakes and ladders'.

3 Ventriloquist and dummy

Work in pairs on a ventriloquist's act. Show the difference between the jerky, mechanical movements of the puppet and the more fluid movements of his human operator. Of course, in this act, the dummy can speak his *own* lines, while the operator mimes 'speaking' with straight lips!

4 Games

Working in pairs or small groups, play a board game, a card game, or game of dexterity (like pick-a-stick). Play as if for real even though working with imaginary pieces.

We should be able to tell what the game is and who is winning or losing!

Developments

Help! Set the scene in a place where a number of interesting objects may be found, i.e. the attic, a scrapyard, a sunken ship, a sale room, a Viking or Egyptian burial chamber, etc.

Start working individually. Look around and choose some small object to take away from the site. Chat in character with other 'explorers' and compare 'treasures'. When you were on the site you saw something that was too big for one person to carry. Find a friend to help you bring out that object. You may both have seen the same thing, or may have to decide whose 'treasure' to collect. Continue to discuss and compare the things that are brought from the site and, at this stage, start to arrange them as an exhibition. Now go back for something that takes four people to carry it. *Agree* between pairs which object is to be brought back. Show it and describe it to the rest of the group and add it to the objects on show. Repeat with eight people finding a 'treasure', and finish with the whole group agreeing on the last and largest item that is to be retrieved.

All the items are now 'on display'. Choose a few curators/guides/ newsmen/policemen (depending on your situation) to talk about the exhibits. If they forget about certain things, members of the group may prompt, 'I'm particularly interested in the pianola behind the billiard table', etc.

Remember, the essence of this impro is *working together* and making *mutual* decisions.

Putting together again Work together in a large group as 'all the king's horses and all the king's men' trying to 'put Humpty together again'. What will happen if you succeed?

Two of a kind Create an improvisation about two people who, because of the nature of the job in hand, must work very closely together. Their lives may depend on mutual co-operation.

Suggest 2 mountaineers, 2 astronauts, 2 deep sea divers, 2 burglars, 2 smugglers, 2 people lost in inhospitable country, 2 bomb disposal officers, 2 circus performers.

Two as one Create a country inhabited only by 2-headed, thick-bodied people. Use the techniques practised in the 'Two as one' exercises.

Send a 'Gulliver' or a party of single-headed explorers to visit the country. How are they received? Are there any lessons to be learned from the two-headed people? What are the advantages/disadvantages of having two heads?

Practical sequences that demand close cooperation, requiring mutual decision-making, concentration and commitment.

1 Help

(a) **Carrying things in pairs** Working with a partner, pick up and carry a long pole, a large pane of glass, a high stack of eggs.

Use slow motion as a control factor and to allow maximum eye communication between partners.

Repeat, setting a perilous, zig-zag, icy pathway along which the objects must be carried. Proceed with extreme caution! There must be no damage!

(b) **Working in fours** Pick up and carry a telegraph pole. A huge pane of glass. Fold an enormous sheet. Pull a car out of a ditch.

Repeat, with all communication in sign language.

(c) **Putting together again!** Work in pairs. A and B. A carries something that is made up of many parts – a completed jigsaw on a tray, a string of beads, a file of loose papers, a feather pillow, a basket of apples. He drops it and the contents scatter. B comes to his aid and helps him to pick up all the pieces and re-assemble them.

2 Two as one

Work in pairs.

(a) **Tying string** Give everyone in the group a short piece of string. Stand side by side in pairs, one holding string in his right hand, the other holding string in left hand. Put free arm around each other's back. You are now *one person* and must tie the two pieces of string together in a firm knot!

(b) **Putting on a coat** Using the same technique (two people linked as one), put on an imaginary coat, walk to the bus stop, get on the bus, pay for your ticket, arrive at work, take off coat, start work, take a coffee break, etc.

(c) **Shared speech** Speak alternate words to make a sentence. Try to talk fluently so that you sound like one person.

Meet another pair and have a conversation with them (or rather, with the composite person).

Problems!   Work in groups of about six. Each person decides *who* he is, and *what* is his particular expertise, e.g.

Mary: teacher – speaks fluent French
Alex: tightrope walker – superb balance and head for heights
Anna: deep-sea diver – strong swimmer
John: mechanic – understands cars.

They find themselves together faced with a problem, e.g.

How to get the grand piano upstairs
How to raise £1000 for a project
How to escape from a cave with the tide coming in
How to get a car across the river (no bridge)
How to erect and decorate a 14 metre Christmas tree

They must pool their talents to find a solution. Share the ideas to see how different personalities cope with the same problem.

Desert island   Work in spontaneous improvisation in 2 or 4 groups.

Presume that the groups are shipwrecked on different parts of a desert island. They need to find shelter, food, warmth, to make plans for escape or rescue, to cope with problems as they arise (wild animals, hurricane, plague of flies, sickness).

Each group should work separately to establish character and relationships within the group. Just as they are beginning to come to terms with the problems, contrive that 2 groups meet. Can they combine forces to make life easier for themselves?

Finally, see what happens if the 4 groups are united. Are they able to work together for the common good?

Discuss reactions, successful cooperative ventures, failures in communication, leadership struggles, etc.

3 Passing buckets!

Work in groups of 6 or 8. Set the problem: you have as many buckets as there are members in your team. The river runs along one side of the room. The street, on the opposite side of the room, is on fire! Find the most efficient method of filling and passing the buckets to put out the fire.

Set a time limit in which groups must solve the problem. Then watch their efforts and decide which would be most use in the emergency!

Developments in improvisation

Lighting a fuse   Consider variations on the 'Lighting a fuse' theme – landslide, avalanche, the domino theory. Work in slow motion to maintain sensitivity and clarity.

Create group improvisations using parallel situations involving people – bankruptcy in big business, a sequence of events leading to a road accident, an arms race, the nursery rhyme:

For the want of a nail the horsehose was lost
For the want of a horseshoe the horse was lost
For the want of a horse the rider was lost
For the want of a rider the battle was lost
For the want of a battle the war was lost
And because of the war the kingdom was lost
For the want of a horseshoe nail.

Reaction in character   Work in groups.

Every member of the group should adopt a different attitude to the given topic, e.g. in a stables you might have the wealthy owner, a disappointed jockey, someone who is allergic to horses, a vet, a horsethief, etc.

Develop in improvisation.

Object with magical properties   Work as a planned improvisation in groups.

Have a collection of interesting small props – a coloured bottle, a feather, a coin, a hat, a glove. Each group takes a 'magic object' and makes up a story about how they acquire it, how they discover that it has magic properties, and what happens to them because of it.

Exercises to establish the habit of give and take in improvisation – the readiness to keep an open mind and accept and develop ideas rather than holding to a preconceived notion.

1 Passing it on

Sit in a circle.

(a) **Lighting a fuse**   Let a touch travel along the line, as flame along a fuse. When it reaches the last person (the explosive) – BOOM! – everyone explodes in sound and movement!

(b) **Touch messages**   Hold hands. Eyes closed. Pass a signal by squeezing a short rhythm into the right hand of one person in the circle, who passes it on through his or her left hand to the next person, and so on round the circle till it gets back to where it started. Has the signal changed?

Send a series of signals at short intervals. What about a word in Morse code?

Have signals travelling clockwise and anti-clockwise.

(c) **Infectious circles**   Pass a sound round the circle – a hiss, a laugh, a sniff, a clicking sound, a yawn. When the sound has passed right round the circle, the next person changes it to something else.

Set a theme for the infectious circle sounds – animal noises, spooks, outer space.

Pass a gesture round the circle – a shrug, a smile, a scratch, a grimace.

Pass gesture and sound. Work positively and quickly so there is no break in the flow of sound and movement.

2 Passing imaginary objects

Work in a circle.

(a) **Continuous action**   Start with a large piece of cake, an ice-cream or bag of sweets or chips. Pass it round the circle, everyone taking a bite or lick until the last person has to make do with the last crumb. Try passing chewing gum!

Blow up a balloon, puff by puff, around the circle. When the balloon is blown up, continue, letting the air out. Add sound.

Use slow motion to deepen the sensation and as a control factor.

Increase the number of 'objects' travelling round the circle.

(b) **Different reactions**   Choose something to pass around the circle – a kitten, a jewel, a photograph, a baby. Each person reacts differently – curiosity, pleasure, nonchalance, greed, amusement, embarrassment, etc.

Personification Work in small groups. Start by sitting in a circle and passing round an imaginary object. As you handle the object, you all take on its characteristics and 'become' whatever you have been holding – old boots, digital watches, Christmas trees. Talk and begin to improvise in character. Where are you? Why are you there? What has happened or is about to happen to you?

Or, begin the sequence by working in pairs. Choose an object each. Now have a conversation in character. Do you have anything in common? Are you likely to get on together? Join another pair and chat in character. As you meet 'objects' that have something in common with you, become a 'collection'. Develop in spontaneous improvisation.

Work in pairs as two similar objects, e.g.

two washing machines in the launderette discussing their clients and the trials of the day;

two houses next door to each other commenting on their occupants and their life styles;

two fir trees in the forest discussing the problems of wind, weather, wild life, and contemplating the future.

Suggest class-conscious objects!

a Rolls and an old banger

two carrier bags from different ends of the market

real pearls and fakes

Try a car telling its life history, or the different rooms in a house reminiscing. Here you might want to use a flashback technique. (See Earliest memories, p. 105.)

Allow a machine to talk about its operator and the conditions of work – a typewriter, a vacuum cleaner, a car. What happens when the machines go on strike?

Encourage use of sounds and speech in reactions.

Pass different things in opposite directions – a cat and a mouse, a hedgehog and a balloon, an energetic dog and a box of eggs. What happens when they meet?

(c) **Reaction in character** Now each person in the circle assumes a character.

You may ask questions (age, occupation, dress, opinions) to aid characterisation.

Pass the 'object' round. As each person handles it, he reacts in character.

This is a subtle development of Different reactions. When the object has passed round the circle, ask people *who* their neighbour was or, better still, sustain the characterisations and chat in character.

(d) **Changing weight and size** This time the object becomes heavier or bigger, or smaller each time it is passed on. Try ball shapes and box shapes before moving on to objects.

Note the activity, *'Double it!'*, which may be worked 'passing it on' in a circle grouping, as above, or with one or two people running through the complete action, for instance:

Working individually, begin a simple mimed action – peeling an apple, reading the newspaper. Then 'Double it!' so that the object becomes twice the size. Double again and again so the actions are huge. Return to normal as you 'Half it!' until the object has disappeared.

Work in pairs, unpacking a box of groceries, playing a board game, sawing a log. Encourage sound and talk.

You'll find that, as the objects become larger, speech becomes slower. Discourage shouting by requiring partners to enunciate very clearly as if communicating across vast distances.

(See Shopping lists, p. 26.)

Once this exercise is accepted, use 'Double It!' to inject vitality into any limber-type activity that seems to be flagging. This is particularly useful with an inhibited older group.

(e) **Total change** The object changes in mid-air as it is passed on, so a mouse may become a violin. The violin may become a newspaper, and so on round the circle.

3 Building descriptions and stories

(a) **Collective descriptions** Sit in a circle. One person begins, e.g. 'Look at that crack in the floor.' He may lean forward for a closer look. The others copy. The next person continues, 'There's smoke coming out of it.' Reaction to smoke. Third person continues, 'It's opening up.' Fourth person, 'And there's something coming out of it.' And so on.

Instant story   Sit in a circle. The first person says the first word of the story. The second adds another, and so on. Whoever mentions a character must move into the centre of the circle to 'become' that character, and must react whenever he is mentioned. If someone introduces '3 witches' or '7 cats' count around the circle for the required number. Limit 'block bookings' to suit the size of your group! Continue until there is just one storyteller left. He must finish the story.

Use this technique with fairy stories, animal stories and melodramas.

Dreams   Start as for Instant story – one word each round the circle. Your finished story is 'the dream'!

Now split into three groups. One group will act out the dream, another will aim to interpret it, while the third re-creates the evening that led up to the dream.

All groups work independently and finally watch each other's interpretations!

Take a line   Sit in a circle. One person moves into the centre of the circle. Another is quietly given a line, which will be the opening line in their conversation, e.g.

> Whatever are you doing here?
> Excuse me, St Peter, I can't open the gate ...
> Did you know, there's £100, in silver, on your doorstep?
> You can't go dressed like that!
> Look, do you want to borrow my handkerchief?
> Is this the place?
> At last, I've found you ...

The other must accept it and react immediately as he thinks fit. Other people from the circle can be brought in, or join in, to develop the spontaneous improvisation.

Everyone should accept what has been said before and build on the description accordingly. Encourage reactions to smell, texture, taste, size, etc.

(b) **Absurd starters** Sit in a circle. One person begins with a deliberately absurd statement, e.g. 'Look at that ant riding a bicycle.' The 6thers continue the story, accepting what has been said and adding their own absurd comments. Encourage movement and group involvement in the story.

(See also Journeys, p. 118.)

---

4 Paper balls

(a) Working individually, roll up a piece of newspaper into a small ball. Hold it, hidden, in your hands. As you open your hands it will 'become' something - a small animal or bird, a vegetable, a treasure - ancient, modern or in the future. Show whatever it is you have to another person. Find out about their 'treasure' and tell them about yours. You can swap objects if you like.

(b) Sit in a circle. Working individually, roll, twist or fold a piece of newspaper to represent an object, plant form or creature. Introduce the group, formally, as guests on a television programme and work round the circle giving each guest a few seconds to explain what he has brought into the studio. Develop with longer interviews, and features on interesting items.

(c) Work in groups of 6. Sit in circles. Place some crumpled paper in the centre of each circle. Members of the group look at it for a while and then begin to put forward ideas about what it could be. This should be done in natural conversation with each member accepting what has been said before and building on that information (as in *Collective descriptions*, p. 149). For example:

A. Do you think it's alive?
B. Yes, it's alive. I can see it breathing.
C. Look, you can see it's got purple feet.
D. Webbed like a duck's.
E. And its head is wet.
F. Could it have come out of the lake?

(d) Work as for (c) but now tell the class that your are going to select one person in each group who covets the 'object' and wants to gain possession of it, and another who feels threatened by it and would like to see it destroyed, though he hasn't the courage to do this himself. All groups close eyes. Touch the ones who covet on the shoulder, the ones who fear on the head. You can deliberately add interest to the issue by touching two who covet, or two who fear, in the same group! Eyes open and start the sequence. At the end, discuss whether the selected pair were

Headlines impro   You will need

(i) a number of headlines from newspapers or magazines, suitable as *titles* for plays

(ii) a number of *'clues'* – i.e. piece of a map/strip of film/torn photograph/bit of print in a foreign language/any small interesting items

(iii) a quantity of snippets from advertising copy, headlines, etc. that could be part of the *dialogue* of the scene.

Divide into groups. Give two or three *titles* to each group and allow them to choose which one they want to use. Let them start to plan the play. After about five minutes, feed in a couple of *clues* per group, which must be incorporated into the storyline. Let the groups continue to plan. Now feed in one *line* for each member of the group which must be spoken as part of his dialogue. Allow the groups to plan and rehearse almost to 'performance pitch'. Now feed in a further *line* each, and allow only a minute or so for these to be incorporated into the play.

Watch the scenes, using this format to introduce each scene:

Group stands in a line. Title is given. Clues are shown. Each member of the group speaks his two set lines clearly and without expression. Group into starting positions. Freeze. Begin.

recognised and whether they achieved their objects. Discuss the methods of persuasion they employed. Sometimes these can be devious! For instance, the one who covets might pretend to protect the one who fears by taking the object away, thus gaining possession of it.

(Bear in mind that this Paper ball sequence could well be worked when you are using paper for other exercises. For instance, Reading in character and situation, p. 85; Dexterity, p. 167.)

5 Take a chair

(a) **Working individually** sit in a chair and let it become a big, soft armchair, a lumpy, scratchy armchair, a deck-chair, an electric chair, a chair on the Big Wheel, a dentist's chair, a ducking stool, etc.

Sit as if you are very young, your own age, very old.

(b) **Working in pairs or small groups** take a chair. Let it become a prison, a baby's playpen, a space ship, a boat, a giant's saucepan, a new invention, a musical instrument, etc.

6 Story circles

Sit in a circle

(a) **Fortunately/unfortunately** First person starts by making a statement, e.g. 'My car's in for a service today.' The second person must begin his related statement with 'fortunately' – 'Fortunately my neighbour gave me a lift to work.' Next person must begin 'unfortunately' – 'Unfortunately his car broke down on the way.' And so on, round the circle.

(b) **No, you didn't** First person begins with a statement, e.g. 'I had cornflakes for breakfast this morning.' The second person contradicts him, 'No, you didn't!' the third person must put himself in number one's shoes, *accept* the contradiction and amend the original statement, 'You're quite right, we'd run out of cornflakes. I had porridge.' Fourth person contradicts, 'No you didn't!' Fifth person picks up from number three and accepts the contradiction, 'Of course, I was so late I caught the train without any breakfast.' Sixth person, 'No you didn't!' Seventh person, 'Yes, the trains weren't running, so I caught a bus.' And so on.

(c) **Creative lying** One person moves into the centre of the circle as the interrogator. He points to someone in the circle and starts with a question, 'Why were you late this morning?' That person replies with a far-fetched excuse, 'There were Apache Indians in our back garden ...'

Games

One-word story   Stand in a circle. One person claps a steady rhythm – a clap followed by a silent beat works well. The first person in the circle says the first word of the story on the first clap. Second person says the second word on the second clap. And so on. If someone can't think of a word, or comes in late, he sits down and listens until the end of the game. Continue until only one person is left to finish the story.

The broom game   Sit in a circle. Pass round a broom, or a shorter length of wood – perhaps a ruler. Each person must use the broom as something else! The first might use it as a crutch, the second might play it like a double bass, the third might hold it like a microphone, and so on.

The bottle game   Work in small groups. Each group is shipwrecked on a desert island and must make maximum use of limited resources!

Suppose you find one bottle. What could you do with it?

Try one shoe, a hairpin, a car tyre, a flower pot.

Develop the game by asking each group to choose the one item (from the list they have already considered) that will be most use to them on the island.

Compare, discuss and defend the choices!

The interrogator, unmoved, should interject, 'Well?' or 'That's no excuse!' The next person takes over and develops the lie, 'They'd kidnapped my little brother...' The interrogator continues to push for the lie to be extended. 'Is that all! That shouldn't have kept you!' Third person takes over, 'And they were going to feed him to the crocodiles in the fish pond...' And so on with each person making the lie more fantastic!

Developments

Styles of command   Work in pairs. Consider the various techniques people use to get other people to do jobs for them! Choose a task – sweeping the leaves off the path, typing a report, cleaning a room – and try the following styles of command:

authoritarian/no questions/military
apologetic/embarrassed/'I'm sorry to ask you, but ...'
feigning illness/appealing to one's better nature/'I've such a headache – would you be an angel ...
circumlocuted, so that the simple order is lost in a morass of irrelevant detail
sneering/undermining/'Try and do a better job than last time.'
the 'one of the boys' line/'We've got to put our backs into this ...'
bullying/threatening
the impossible master who can't explain what he wants and is never satisfied
the master with natural authority

Discuss experiences and the effectiveness of each style of command.

Who is the master?   Work in pairs or small groups on a planned improvisation in which the one who would appear to be subservient is really the dominant character, e.g.

small child and harassed mother
civil servant and secretary of state
caretaker and headteacher
female and chauvinistic male, etc.

Passing the buck/Pecking order   Develop an improvisation called Passing the buck or Pecking order, drawing on your own experience and observations made in Chain of command, Styles of command and Who is the master?

Exercises to develop language flow and to create an awareness and critical consideration of servant/master roles in everyday life.

1 Servant/master

(a) Work in pairs. A and B. A is the servant, B the master. B orders his servant to do a job for him – 'Clean my boots!' but before A has time to start that job, B must issue another order – 'Answer the door'! Before the servant can get to the door, there must be another command – 'Put a log on the fire!' And so on. You'll find that 30 seconds of this exercise is long enough even for the most extrovert! Use cymbal control to stop, and always change over so the servant has the chance to become the master.

(b) Work the exercise as above with several servants to one master. The master must keep all his servants occupied, either working in pairs or individually. Set the scene for this 'work force' – restaurant, garage, building site, hospital, school, etc. Or, with young children, dramatise with a 'witch' or 'wizard' ordering 'cats' or 'goblins' to collect ingredients for a spell. If you play the witch, send the goblins on amazing journeys to fetch moondust, or fishes' fins from the bottom of the ocean, etc. Make up a chant as the spell is brewing! See if the charm works!

(c) Work in pairs. A and B. A is the servant, B the master. This time all the master's orders must be concerned with completing one task – mending a bike, arranging a room for a party, planting the garden. Allow about 8 or 10 'orders'. Then B becomes the master and orders that the job be *un*-done, negating the original commands in reverse order.

(d) Work silent servant/master sequences using eye contact and gesture. (See Eye control, p. 29.)

(e) Work in pairs. This more advanced exercise requires more language flow and give-and-take between servant and master. The servant is now looking for an opportunity to ask his master to *assist* him. The master must not block any reasonable request but should anticipate the moment when he'll relinquish his dominant position. The situation is now open for a gradual, mutually accepted role reversal.

2 Chain of command

Stand in groups of four. A, B, C and D. All A's move to one corner of the room, B's to another, etc.

Prepare *written* 'memos' about a job that must be done, and hand one to each member of the A group. Each A reads his memo and *telephones* his second-in-command, B, to pass on the instruction. B listens to the

Distractions   Consider the various ways people distract others in real life. Why do they do it?

From your own observations, and after discussion and experience of the Distraction exercises, create an improvisation on the theme 'Distractions'.

Play some comic scenes – 'Card school in Red River Saloon', 'The television programme I didn't see', 'Snooker tournament' – but also think of the more serious aspects of this topic.

Persuasion   After experience of the Persuasion exercises, develop in discussion and improvisation.

Consider persuasion in   advertising
religion
politics

What qualities must an effective 'persuader' possess?

At what point does persuasion become pressure, manipulation, exploitation, trickery?

What are the 'tricks' of the persuader's trade?

Consider the following adjectives applied to the 'persuaded':
understanding, sympathetic, adaptable, open-minded, impulsive, malleable, gullible, insecure, selfish, greedy, fearful.

And these, applied to the 'persuader':
visionary, missionary, passionate, sincere, knowledgeable, determined, intimidating, underhand, immoral.

instructions and walks to C (third in line) to tell him, *face-to-face*, the task that is set. C then moves on to D and must explain and, if necessary, *demonstrate* what is required. D is the one who will *do* the job! What does he make of the instructions that have been passed down the line?

Feed in a second, and a third, batch of memos to the A group and continue working the sequence allowing less time for communication between C and D.

Evaluate the effectiveness of each chain of command. Discuss the stresses and misunderstandings that are caused.

Change over roles.

3 Persuasion

Work with a partner. A and B.

(a) A clenches his fists. B must talk to A and persuade him to open his hands and relax. Use language only in the first instance. Repeat, employing gentle touch at the right moment. Change over.

(b) Both think of a number, or a colour, a name, a tree, a place, etc. A tries to persuade B to prefer his choice to his own. Change over.

(c) Choose a topic you feel strongly about. A aims to win B over to his way of thinking. Change over.

(d) Try to sell your partner something. A is a door-to-door salesman, selling anything from floor polish to luxury swimming pools! He should decide what he is going to sell, then tap on A's door and try his luck!

Discuss the styles of persuasion that work best and the factors that contribute to acceptance of persuasion.

4 Talk your partner down

Work in pairs. A and B.

(a) Both of you talk at once about anything that comes into your heads. Keep eye contact with each other. The one who falters first is the loser! Try again!

(b) A starts and must keep talking so that B can't get a word in. When B manages to say something, the sequence stops. A does not try to shout him down. Change over.

(c) Now both partners are aiming to talk each other down, but with the mutual understanding that dominance will pass from one to the other.

(d) Work this exercise in gibberish.

Game

The Court of the Holy Dido   Sit in a circle. Choose a 'President of the Court of the Holy Dido' and place in front of him 'the Holy Dido' (a rolled-up newspaper). Everyone else is referred to as 'Brother' or 'Sister'. They all sit cross-legged and motionless.

The object of the game is to retain the sense of exaggerated deference to the President and his venerable court. No one may move or speak without first asking permission of the President, and no frivolous behaviour (giggling, yawning, etc.) is permitted.

If a brother sees another move or smile, he may ask permission to administer punishment to the offending brother with the holy Dido. He must address all his comments, with the most fastidious courtesy, to the President. First he asks permission to stand, then he continues,

'I crave permission to administer punishment to Brother Michael who has dared to smile/un-cross his legs/scratch/smirk/raise an eyebrow in the most august court of the Holy Dido.'

The President nods agreement and, without emotion, holds up as many fingers as the offender will receive 'lashes'. The accuser then asks permission to pick up the Holy Dido. He asks the President to give permission for the accused to stand, and may then administer the punishment (to the offender's rump!). There must be no reaction from the rest of the court! Permission is requested before the two brothers can sit down again.

And so on! Any brother who is deemed to be discourteous to the President (by forgetting to ask permission) may be censured by another brother.

If the President's behaviour is in any way reprehensible he may be challenged by a brother who then takes over as President.

The game finishes when the President declares the Court of the Holy Dido well and truly closed!

5 Distraction

Work in pairs. A and B.

(a) A starts a task that requires some degree of concentration, e.g. saying the alphabet, counting in twos or fives, saying every other word of a nursery rhyme, etc. B tries to distract him so that he makes a mistake or loses his place. B may do anything except touch A! Change over.

(b) Add a physical aspect to A's task – an easy dance step while saying the alphabet, laying cards down in a pattern while counting in twos, etc. B aims to distract A but still may not touch him.

(c) Hand out some pieces of newspaper. A begins to read a passage aloud. B interrupts to ask him questions: 'Do you know what the time is?' 'What's for lunch?' etc. A must answer each question and immediately return to reading his paper, without losing his place or the gist of the story. Change over.

(d) Work (a), (b) and (c) in a circle grouping with one person in the centre concentrating on his task while the others try to distract him.

6 Nice and nasty

Sit in a circle.

(a) **Compliments all round** First person says somethig complimentary about the person on his right. Next person says something complimentary about him. And so on round the circle.

(b) **Nice and nasty** First person says something nice about the person on his right and something nasty about the person on his left. And so on round the circle. So everyone has something nice and something nasty said about them.

All comments should be received dead pan without question or argument.

7 Building up and taking down

(a) Work with a partner. A and B. Presume that A has not seen his friend, B, for a while. When they meet, A is going to 'build up' B by telling him how good he looks, that he's heard how well he's doing in work, etc. B accepts the compliments and chats with A, taking over and developing the role that A is presenting for him. Change over.

(b) Work as for (a) but now A is aiming to 'take down' B. 'You do look tired!'/'Pity you didn't get the job...'/'Have you tried the new acne

Developments in improvisation and discussion

Create a scene (prepared impro, mime, verse readings, dance-drama) to illustrate one of the following well-known quotations:

Man was born free and everywhere he is in chains.

Jean Jacques Rousseau

I am His Highness' dog at Kew;
Pray tell me, sir, whose dog are you?

Alexander Pope

There must always be a master and servants in all civilized communities, for it is natural, and whatever is natural is right.

J. M. Barrie
('The Admirable Crichton')

If thou art a master, sometimes be blind;
If a servant, sometimes be deaf.

Thomas Fuller

Great fleas have little fleas
Upon their backs to bite 'em;
And little fleas have lesser fleas,
And so on ad infinitum.

Augustus de Morgan

He who serves two masters has to lie to one.

Portuguese Proverb

No man is good enough to be another's master.

George Bernard Shaw
('Major Barbara')

cream? It cleared up John's spots. Might do the same for you,' etc. B must accept and develop the depressing picture that A is painting for him.

(c) Work similar exercises with one person allowing himself to be built up or taken down by a group. Change the 'victim' frequently and always allow time for discussion after such a sequence. Note the physical reaction to praise and censure, flattery and insult.

8 Building and destruction cycle

Work in pairs. A and B. A builds something, carefully and proudly, in mime - perhaps, a structure in playing cards or matches. B watches closely and, when his partner has completed the task, B destroys it. B now relents and starts to rebuild the structure, remembering how A went about the task. A begins to help him and the structure is finished together.

Development

House for sale   Have a 'family' of 4, and 2 or 4 'prospective buyers'. The family is aiming to sell a house which is precariously balanced on the pinnacle of a mountain! The house has four symmetrical rooms and the point of balance is exactly in the centre. They keep the house level by spreading the load, normally one person per room! When the prospective buyers come to view, they must cooperate as a family to keep the house steady without making their appalling problem obvious.

Everyone else sits around the outside of the house and, if they can see that the house is swaying towards them, they make creaking noises! If the house tilts to the point of no return, it may crash!

Games

Where are you?   Work with a partner. A and B. A's close eyes. B leads A gently around the room, taking care not to bump into any other couples. Stand still. B asks A where in the room he thinks he is. Change over.

How many feet?   Work with a partner. A and B. Stand facing each other at opposite sides of the room. A begins to walk towards B until B calls 'Stop'. A then indicates, by holding up fingers, how many steps (heel to toe) he thinks he will need to complete the 'crossing'. If B thinks he is right, he signals agreement. If he disagrees, he indicates his estimate. A continues to cross. How many steps does he take? Change over.

Exercises to develop confidence by deepening understanding of personal and wider space.

1 Personal orientation

(a) Working individually, begin some simple physical exercise such as skip-jumping on the spot. Continue with eyes closed.

(b) Lie down on the floor. Arms by sides. Eyes closed. To the slow count of ten, lift your arms over your head, in a full semi-circle, so that the backs of your hands rest on the floor. Aim to move arms at a fixed pace. See if hands can touch the floor at the count of ten, no sooner, no later.

(c) Standing up, work a similar exercise raising arms to the side to touch backs of hands above head.

2 Spatial orientation

Individual work
(a) Stand around the outside of the room. Choose a spot on the floor. Assess the distance in your mind first, then go and stand on your chosen spot.

(b) Repeat with eyes closed.

(c) Take five steps away from your spot. Turn. Eyes closed. Walk back to it.

(d) Work as for (c) but return to spot, walking backwards.

Pair work
(e) A and B. Stand opposite sides of the room facing your partner. A's close eyes. A must move forward and stop within an arm's length of B. Move very slowly. B may hum quietly to help his partner. Change over.
   In discussion, after this sequence, pairs may agree on an 'on course' signal (perhaps a steady hum) and other sounds which indicate 'veering to the right' and 'veering to the left'. (See Sound signals, pp. 63–5).

(f) Work a similar sequence, but this time both A and B move forward, so A needs to assess the distance that B will be travelling. Change over.

Games

Paper-ball races　Run team races, blowing or flicking paper balls. For example:

　Each team sits. Front person blows (or flicks) paper ball all the way round the team back to number 2, who takes over, and so on. Penalty points can be issued if any paper ball travels more than 1 metre away from its home team!

Launch pad　Work with a partner. Sit back to back, knees bent, arms linked. Work together to try to raise yourselves onto your feet without releasing arms.

Surfing　Work with a partner. A and B. A lies down, as if a 'breaker'. B 'surfs' over him, so their bodies are at right angles. As soon as B has cleared A, he turns and lies down as a second 'breaker'. A gets up and 'surfs' over B. And so on. Run a 'surfing race' from one side of the room to the other.

Log-rolling　Work in groups of 4 to 8. Lie close together, head to tail, like sardines! First 'log' rolls over the others to the end of the line. Second 'log' follows him. And so on, until the set distance has been covered.

Orientation game

Group Work
Entire group holds hands in a large circle. Eyes closed. Still holding hands, change the circle shape into a square. When the group is satisfied that it is now standing in a square shape, ask those who think they are at the corner points to put up their hands. Eyes open to check.

Run a similar sequence, forming a square into a triangle.

Exercises in awareness and control to promote physical trust within a group. The exercises are definitely non-competitive and should never be practised in a lighthearted or dare-devil manner. They provide essential pre-experience for the games which can incorporate a competitive element.

1 Dexterity

(a) **Making paper balls**   Give everyone a small piece of newspaper. Roll it up into a tight paper ball and, as you do it, say 'R-O-LL', lengthening the vowel until you run out of breath. Squeeze the ball and say 'SQU-E-E-ZE' until you have no more breath. Relax.

(b) **Waterfall**   Working individually, 'waterfall' your paper ball hand-below-hand until it reaches the ground. Aim for smooth, controlled action.

(c) **Toe flicks**   Place your heel on the ground and flick the paper ball with your toe, using first the inside then the outside of your foot. Try with the other leg.
   Work with a partner. A and B. A must flick the ball into the goalmouth (B's feet). Remember – *flick* not kick!

(d) **Breath control**   Crawl on the ground and take the ball for a walk, blowing it along. The ball must be kept close to you and under control throughout the 'walk'!
   Note that this limbering activity could be followed by a creative exercise using the paper balls. (See Paper balls, p. 151.)

2 Balance

(a) Working individually, stand with feet about a third of a metre apart, lift heads, drop shoulders, and feel the strength of this perfectly poised position.

(b) Lift one foot about 80–100 cm off the ground. How far can you take this foot around and away from your other leg without overbalancing?

(c) 'Write' your name with the point of your toe in the air, horizontally then vertically.

(d) **Foot-notes!**   Work with a partner writing messages in the air.
   (See Writing in hands, p. 113).

(e) Work with a partner to discover a variety of ways of supporting each other in perfect balance and control. Choose two examples where support is shared, and two examples each where one is supporting the other.

Climbing the cliff   Work in groups of 3. A, B and C. Imagine the floor of the hall is the vertical cliff-face. A lies down and stretches, as if climbing. B climbs up beside him until his feet are on A's shoulders. C uses A's and B's bodies to help him climb the cliff and 'stands' on B's shoulders. At this point, A starts to climb again until he is resting on C's shoulders. And so on, until they all reach the summit!

Skinning the snake   Work in teams of 5 or 6. Stand behind each other, legs astride. Bend knees and, with one hand, reach between your legs to grasp the free hand of the person behind you. Thus the team is linked, and must remain so! The last person in the team lies down and the others shuffle backwards over his body. The last person but one will now need to lie down, and the team continues to shuffle back over him. And so on until everyone is lying down. An energetic team can now reverse the process! The last one to lie down gets up and 'pulls' the 'skin' back onto the snake.

Sitting circle   Stand in a circle, as if in a circular queue. Put your hands on the waist of the person in front. Shuffle closer together if necessary. Bend knees slowly and sit gently on the knees of the person behind you. Everyone should be sitting. When comfortable balance is achieved, appoint a leader to lead a circular 'ballet'. Work in slow motion, raising left legs, arms, in rounded even movements.

3 Rocking the baby

Work in groups of 3. A, B and C. A and B stand facing each other, no more than a metre apart. C is the 'baby' and stands between them. C closes his eyes, allows himself to lean towards A or B, and is gently rocked backwards and forwards.

4 Willing to fall

Work in groups of 6. Form a tight circle with one person in the middle. That person closes his eyes and slowly allows himself to 'fall' towards the protective circle. The circle supports him and sets him on balance again. Members of the circle now concentrate silently to 'will' him to fall in a certain direction.

5 Floating on the lilo

Work in groups of 4. One person links arms, back-to-back, with another member of the group and lifts him so that he is supported on his back. The other two gently support the legs of the 'floater' who closes his eyes and enjoys this dream-like experience.

6 Safety net

Six people kneel in pairs, facing each other, and clasp hands with their partner opposite, thus forming a 'trough' or 'safety net' into which another person may allow himself to fall. Start with this person falling forwards from a kneeling position, and gradually progress to working with the whole group standing. As confidence grows, it will be possible to take a running jump and 'dive' forward into the safety net. The 'net' should now be able to 'throw' the person over onto his or her back to be lifted shoulder-high and carried around the room.

This exercise demands total trust and must never be rushed or worked in a frivolous atmosphere.

A selection of tag games to channel aggressive energy

Two circle tag   Stand in pairs. A and B. All A's form an inner circle. B's form an outer circle, immediately behind their partners and facing the same way. Someone from the inner circle is chased by someone from the outer circle. The 'pursued' can 'save' himself by standing in front of any pair in the double circle, in which case the outer member of that pair becomes the pursued.

Red Rover   The 'catcher' stands in the middle of the room. He must hop to catch his prey. The rest of the group stands against one wall of the room. At a signal, they run across to the opposite wall. Anyone caught joins the catcher, hopping to catch prey. Play vigorously until there is only one 'victim' left.

British bulldog   Play as for Red Rover, except that the catcher must lift his victim off the ground.

Crocodile tag   Have one catcher who becomes the 'head' of the crocodile. As he catches people they all join hands to form his 'tail'. Only the head can catch, but the tail performs a useful service by isolating and cornering victims!

Fox and goose   Choose a 'fox' and a 'goose'. The rest of the group stands in a circle, hands linked, arms raised to form arches. The goose has a few seconds' start, and runs in and out of the arches and across the circle as he chooses. The fox must follow his path exactly. If he fails to do so, he changes places with someone in the circle. Play until a fox gets the goose.

Cat and mouse   Select a 'cat' and a 'mouse'. The rest of the class stands in a block in evenly-spaced rows. All face the same way. Space so that fingertips just touch your neighbour's fingers. Turn sideways and space in the same way with your new neighbour. Your arms form the 'walls' of the corridors down which the cat and mouse will run. Cat enters at one corner. Mouse at another. They are both restricted to running in the corridors and must not break through 'walls'. At a signal from the teacher, the whole class turns through 90° to touch fingers with their original neighbours, thus creating a new corridor formation. When the mouse is caught, cat and mouse change places with two of the other members of the group.

Exercises based on fighting.

NB All the exercises must be practised in *slow motion* with *sustained eye contact* between partners.

1 Silent scream

Working individually, 'scream' with the whole body, but make no sound. Build 'scream' to the count of ten. Relax to the count of ten. Lie down and relax completely.

2 Mock fights

(a) **Shadow boxing** Working individually, 'shadow box' an imaginary partner.

(b) **Ropeless tug of war** Work with a partner. Lay down an imaginary rope. Feel the rope and grasp it. Agree by eye contact who will win or lose.

Divide into teams and group as if for a tug of war. Remember, there is no contact between the teams and no trial of strength! The teams should work together and allow themselves to win or lose.

(c) **Staves and swords** Work with a partner and 'fight' in slow motion using a stave and then a long sword. The weapons must keep you apart! Do not touch your partner.

(d) **Selecting weapons** Work in pairs, A and B. A watches B select a weapon. In slow motion A attacks B. During the fight the weapon may change hands.

(e) **Delayed reactions** A 'hits' B without touching him. B freezes and then reacts to the pain. Change over.

(f) **Fight sequences** Plan a short fight sequence, with or without weapons. Work in slow motion and limit yourselves to 10 movements which you number 1-10. Count aloud and keep eye contact with each other as you work out the sequence. Develop in units of 10 movements. Use levels and floor contact to add visual interest to the fight. Watch the fight sequences (still in slow motion) and commend physical control, balance and follow-through in movement.

Quick physical reaction games

Slap-happy Stand facing a partner, about a metre apart. Both hold out closed fists in front of you. Together say, 'And...' then any number, 1–5. If different numbers are chosen, nothing happens, but if both choose the same number each tries to slap the other's wrist. The first to slap gains a point.

Knee-boxing Stand facing a partner, knees bent, hands on knees. Each partner tries to slap the other's inside knee as he takes his hand off to 'attack'. Score points for each slap.

3   Clowning

An introduction to stage fighting. Rehearse in slow motion and remember that the one who pretends to be hurt is really in control! Work in pairs. A and B.

(a) **Hair pull**   A places his hand flat on B's head. B presses his own hand down on A's hand, holding it to his head. B is now in control and can jump up and down, drop to his knees, making grimaces and noise as if being hurt. A follows B, with suitable aggression. Note that if B is pretending to be pulled along the floor, he must actually crawl forwards – in reality, pushing A away from him.

(b) **Nose pull and ear pull**   Work a similar sequence with the 'victim' holding his opponent's hand to his face.

(c) **Foot stamp**   A faces B. A raises his knee high and stamps his foot down on the floor to the outside of B's foot. B reacts as if in pain, raising his foot and hopping.

Dramatic motivation   When these techniques have been mastered, add verbal dramatic motivation. Remember, no fight is silent, and it is the facial expression and aggressive noise that gives the sense of reality.

Appendix

Three longer sequences

Essential pre-experience is listed beside the notes – though, obviously, the more experience a group has of working in drama, the more satisfying will be the results.

Please note that the notes are not intended as set lesson plans! Each class and teacher will bring their own interpretations, amendments and additions to our suggested 'scenarios'.

1. *Day and night,* – based on a West African myth has been worked with 9-year-olds and also as a Theatre in Education project with sixth-form and 6-year-olds.

The nibbling away of holes to make the moon and stars is the traditional solution, but there is no reason why your class should not devise an equally acceptable alternative!

Depending on the amount of pre-experience already given, the sequence will take at least 40 minutes.

2. *Ednubid* – a middle school/secondary/adult sequence.

This sequence may be worked in three lessons, or allow at least 1½ hours to run right through. Again, much depends on the experience of the group and the number of stories related.

Ednubid is an interesting introduction to discussion on the growth of legend, as stories and 'evidence' are passed down and interpreted by the generations.

3. *Red, green, blue and purple* – a secondary/adult project.

It should run in one session lasting approximately 2 hours. Various aspects of the sequence can be developed or played down to fit in with the skills and interest of the group.

The main value comes in discussion at the end of the sequence.

1 Day and night

Work in four groups:
  hardworking people on earth
  gods
  animals on earth
  Ananse (a winged spider-like creature, go-between of heaven and earth)
Give pre-experience before children select groups:

Hardworking people
There are so many jobs to do! (Be the master yourself, or appoint a few overlords.) Try working on a fast-moving conveyor belt like a human machine. No let-up!

(See **Servant / Master**, p. 157; **Making machines**, p. 135.)

Gods
They are luxury-loving, idle, and rather bored. Bath in asses' milk, eat grapes, etc.! Float in slow mirrored sequence.

(See **Basic mirror work**, p. 17; **Mirror work to music**, p. 19.)

Animals
Make animal sounds. Motivate sounds. Move as animals.

(See **Animals**, p. 81.)

Ananse
Make spiders with eight legs! For the purpose of this story in which Ananse has to move fairly quickly, it's probably easier to work in pairs. (There's no reason why you shouldn't have more than one spider!)

(See **Spiders and starfish**, p. 132; **Two as one**, p. 142.)

Select groups. Arrange gods (preferably on a raised area), Ananse(s) at the feet of the gods, people and animals in the main working area. They all make themselves at home in their areas, grouping into family or work groups.

All the action of the story runs simultaneously.

The problem is that there is no night. It's always daylight and the people are exhausted.

Begin to run the sequence with people working, gods relaxing, Ananse(s) looking on.

Brief Ananse that as soon as he sees a number of people yawning he should go to see what is the matter with them.

They will tell him the problem, which he relates to the gods. The gods will probably not take a lot of notice!

Ananse returns to earth. He has an idea. If the gods can hear the people and animals yawning, they might take pity. Everyone yawns.

(See **Infectious circles,** p. 147.)

If the gods take notice, all well and good! If not, Ananse may have to 'collect' the yawns in his wings and take them up for the gods to hear.

(See **Repeated sound circles,** p. 69.)

Everyone, even the smallest animal, yawns into Ananse's wings. When the yawn is released, the mass sound is repeated.

What can the gods do? How do you get rid of light? Turn it off? - can't do that! Draw the curtains - cover it up? Yes! But what with?

Maybe the gods, who are a little bored, would make a cloth - a large cloth! If they agree, work commences (spinning, weaving, knitting, sewing together).

(See **Help!,** p. 142.)

Ananse goes to tell the people and animals that their problem will be solved. Meanwhile they keep working.

The cloth is finished and the gods heave it over the earth. Complete darkness!

How can the people find their way home in blackness? Eyes shut (to indicate the darkness) they try to finish their jobs and make their way home.

(See **Leading the blind,** p. 115.)

The animals are afraid and make fearful noises.

The gods heave off the cloth. Ananse comes down again. What's the matter? Don't they like the darkness? Too sudden? Too black. What can be done?

Could the gods move the cloth in slow motion? Action from the gods. People are happier, but it's still pitch black.

What is the answer? Maybe some holes could be scratched or nibbled in the cloth?

Who will do it? Appointed animals set to work - and create the pattern of the moon and stars. Everyone is pleased - and tired!

The gods slowly heave the sky cloth over for the last time that day and everyone sleeps.

2 Ednubid: past into present

1 Start in groups of 6 or 8.

Long ago, tribespeople were sitting around their fires working – making utensils, implements, clothes, weapons, traps and charms .... Show your neighbour what you have made and describe how it will be used.

(See Copy the expert, p. 21.)

Begin to work together on larger projects for the benefit of the tribe.

(See Help!, p. 142.)

A messenger arrives with news of the death of your leader, EDNUBID. You must make a long journey to pay your tributes.

(See Different ways of walking, p. 51; Journeys, p. 118.)

As all the tribespeople draw near to the sacred clearing or temple where Ednubid's body is lying in state, begin a mournful ritual chant. And, eventually, sit, eyes closed, in a large ceremonial circle.

(See Atmospheric chants, p. 68; Repeated sound circles, p. 69.)

You will be handed objects – important possessions and symbols of your leader – which must be passed round the circle. (You will need 6 or 8 objects of varying shapes, weights and textures – the stranger the better.)

(See Blind detectives, p. 118; Awareness of texture, p. 119.)

The objects are passed round and felt by the tribespeople who allow the shape and feel of the object to conjure an image or story of their dead leader. Tribespeople may make any sound they wish while handling the objects.

Collect in the objects and allow tribespeople to open eyes. The tribespeople move back into their groups to mourn their leader by remembering aspects of his or her character or incidents they remember, prompted by the objects they have handled.

Each tribesperson tells a story relating to Ednubid. As it is told, the scribes in the group write the essence of the story in hieroglyphics or draw primitive pictures to illustrate salient points. (Have a number of piles of rough paper and crayons about the room and collect up drawings when they are done.)

The tribespeople gather again, chanting in happier tone, and tell, or mime to a commentary, the chosen stories of Ednubid.

(See Sound patterns, p. 91; Rounds, p. 91; Running commentaries, p. 79.)

2 The time is now the present day.

Regroup into 3s or 4s. You are archeologists and historians who have discovered remains, including illustrated fragments, relating to the ancient tribe of Ednubid. (Distribute the hieroglyphics and pictures torn into pieces.) From this evidence you should be able to assess how the tribe lived.

Shortly you will be appearing on television to expound your theories and give your professional opinions. One or two may not speak English and an interpreter may be employed.

(See Interpreters, p. 82.)

It seems unlikely that the experts will agree, and Ednubid remains a mystery!

3　Tomorrow is Ednubid's Day!

Divide into 3 teams, representing the village pubs: The Red Cow, The Black Bull, and The Dog and Duck. Every year you vie with each other to produce the most amusing and spectacular commemoration of Ednubid's Day.

Statues are built. Each pub has a special Ednubid's Day greeting. There are tableaux, dances, songs, processions, and always a competition to finish (the Ednubid's head relay, Pin the smile on Ednubid, etc.)

(See Sculpting, p. 121; Group statues, p. 126; Handshakes, p. 109; Walking in rhythm, p. 53; and general experience of Games.)

During the planning, local television may visit your pub to find out how your preparations are going.

(See Cameraman, p. 33.)

Celebrate Ednubid's Day! At the close of the day, the Lady Mayoress will present the Ednubid trophy to the winning pub!

As a conclusion to this sequence you may like to build a composite class statue in Ednubid's honour. This could be done a week or so after working the sequence to discover the points about Ednubid that stick in the memory!

3 Red, green, blue and purple

An extended improvisation based on colour groups.

You're all at a party. Mix and find out what people are eating and drinking.

(See all exercises in **Colour**, pp. 8–11; **Parties**, p. 111.)

Freeze! Choose one of these colours: RED, GREEN, BLUE or PURPLE – and find some ruse to bring your chosen colour into your conversation. Spend longer chatting to people who seem to share your colour preference.

Split into four groups according to colour choice. (These will not be of equal size. In our experience, Reds will be the largest group, Greens and Blues about equal, Purples considerably smaller.)

(Hand out Character brief cards A1, A2, A3, A4 – one to each group.)

Each group is now going to make up a national anthem or chant. (During the chant rehearsals aim to mark everyone with their chosen colour – a stick-on label or a dab of water-based make up.)

When chants are ready, position each clan in one corner of the room and have a chant battle!

(See **Chant battle**, p. 57.)

Clans return to territories. You must now prepare a television documentary about your clan and area. This may take the form of a series of interviews with people in your clan (*Down our way*), a guided tour around landmarks in your territory indicating their history and present use, an advert persuading people that your region is the place to be, etc.

Watch the programmes.

If necessary, return to territories.

(Hand out Character brief 2, closely followed by Instructions C1, C2, C3 and C4. These instructions are guidelines only. They are probably best given verbally, and should be adapted to reflect what you have discovered about the groups and areas. Their purpose is to promote interaction and a certain independence among groups.

Now announce that a new motorway scheme is to cut through the area. Distribute a map showing the proposed route.)

How will this motorway affect you? Discuss with friends and associates.

A public meeting is called. Each clan should appoint a spokesperson to air their views, and then the meeting will be thrown open to the floor.

Return to your own territories to discuss the meeting.

Interrupt discussion with a vitally important radio message – something like this: 'For some time this country has faced the threat of nuclear war.

In view of heightening tension the Government is providing every clan with an equal amount of anti-radioactive-fallout material – ARAFOM. If a body, or group of bodies, is completely surrounded or covered with ARAFOM there is nothing to fear. Note that ARAFOM must be placed on floor as well as all sides to be effective. The makers suggest that personal experiments are conducted to find the most agreeable and efficient methods of employing ARAFOM. Remain calm. There is no immediate danger.'

ARAFOM – equal-sized piles of newspaper – is distributed. Note that the same amount of newspaper is given to each group, regardless of the number of people in the group.

Let the sequence develop in spontaneous improvisation. Groups attempt to organise themselves and may interact as they choose.

(See **Problems!**, p. 144; **Desert island,** p. 144; **Passing buckets!,** p. 145.)

Interrupt with announcement of imminent nuclear strike. You have five minutes to build your shelters. To finish, count down 10–1.

Explosion. Darkness and silence.

Sit in the debris and discuss.

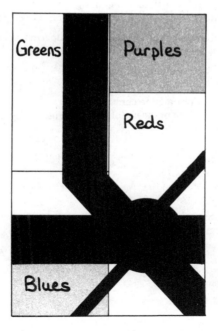

Map showing territories and proposed motorway

Cards A1, A2, A3 and A4 (make one of each)

Reds   like to be in the centre of things, energetic, attractive, lack subtlety, can be ruthless

Greens   rural, hard-working, introspective, survivors

Blues   dreamers, innovators, mystics

Purples   fashionable, luxury-loving, influential, eccentric

Card B (make four)

Reds look down on Greens, can't understand Blues, envy Purples.
Greens accept (but do not respect) Purples and Blues; are suspicious of Reds.
Blues have affinity with Purples and Greens, but find it difficult to get on with Reds.
Purples are amused by Blues, protective towards Greens, and frightened by Reds.

Instructions C1, C2, C3 and C4 (Relevant information to each group)

A Red needs to employ a Blue artist/designer/writer.
Another Red wants to develop a country club in Green country.

A Green wants to sell his produce in a Red supermarket chain.
Another Green is looking for Purple support for a conservation scheme.

A Blue wants a Red commercial backer for his work.
Another Blue is in love with a Purple.

A Purple wants to join a Blue commune.
Another Purple needs to make use of shooting rights over Green country.